Flower Arranging

Flower Arranging

Introduction by John Clayton,
The Royal Horticultural Society

We wish to thank The Royal Horticultural
Society for their cooperation in the
preparation of this book, and the verification
of horticultural information contained in it.

Editor: Elsie Burch Donald

Designers: Mike Rose
                 Demetrakis Kourdoulou

Authors: Judy Allen
                 Charlotte Edwards
                 Iain Finlayson
                 Anne Johnson
                 Rosemary Lamont

Photographers: Steve Bicknell
                 Jon Harris
                 Herbie Schmitz

**Planned, edited and designed by
Tigerlily Limited,
34 Marshall Street, London W1**

First published 1979 by Octopus Books Limited
59 Grosvenor Street, London W1

© 1979 Octopus Books Limited

ISBN 0 7064 0984 1

Printed in Italy by New Interlitho S.p.A. - Milan

Contents

Introduction

As will be seen from the introductory chapter of this book, the art of flower arranging in its widest sense is of very ancient origin, dating back as far as the ancient Egyptian stone reliefs and wall paintings, through the Greek and Roman periods, the Renaissance and on to Victorian times. By the middle of the 20th century, even in our highly industrialized modern society and after two world wars, the popularity of flower arranging is greater than ever before, confined to no one nation or class, and universal in its variety and appeal.

The reason for this appeal is not hard to find. Flower arrangement can be practised by anyone, whether professionally or as a purely amateur activity. Many arrangers belong to one of the groups and societies which flourish world wide and have done so much to promote and encourage interest in flower arranging as a hobby. The elaborate and massive professional arrangements, made to set off a society wedding in a cathedral or a great city banquet, may impress by their very size and splendour; but the child's bouquet of primroses and spring flowers, brought in to its mother, is in its own way just as sincere an expression of the art, and an early interest thus developed can remain as an enjoyable activity throughout one's life.

In this book will be found a comprehensive survey, not only of the history of flower arranging but of the related practical aspects such as the selection and care of flowers, the materials and equipment available and methods of preserving; as well as of ideas for arrangements both for special occasions and for everyday enjoyment in the home.

One important aspect brought out by the book is that to enjoy arranging flowers it is not necessary to have a large estate or to buy expensive, out-of-season material from the florist. Useful practical advice is given on a wide range of beautiful flowers and foliage which can be grown in most gardens, and there are hints on their special treatment as well as suggestions for possible uses of some of our wild flowers, grasses and trees.

The criticism is sometimes made that the art of flower arranging is being too greatly formalized by the development of strict rules and conventions. This book should encourage all those who love flowers to experiment, to use their imagination and to take full advantage of the great wealth of material available to us.

John Clayton

The Royal Horticultural Society

A Short History

There are few written references to western-style flower arranging beyond the past hundred years and, in the absence of much direct, detailed evidence, we may safely assume that the art is a comparatively recent innovation and defined principles have evolved only through the work of modern practitioners. That such a fugitive decorative art should have gone largely unrecorded is perhaps appropriate to its character, but research into the wider history of flowers and of painting provides clues which, taken together, form some evidence about changing fashions in flower decoration.

Taken as a whole, western flower arranging is mainly the evolution of a massed 'bouquet' style. A linear style, Ikebana, originated in Japan centuries ago, but it did not influence western methods until the early years of the twentieth century. (The origins and development of Ikebana are described in chapter seven.)

Early History

Ancient Egyptian stone reliefs and wall paintings not only use the lotus flower as decoration, but occasionally show the blossoms (actually those of the blue water lily, *Nymphaea caerulea*, or the larger white *Nymphaea lotus*) placed in narrow tripartite mouths of terracotta jars. No attempt is made to soften the lines of the flowers or to combine them with other plant material, and 'arrangement' seems too strong a word for the display.

It is safe to say that cut flowers were unknown in ancient Greece, although an olive branch is known to have been placed in a jar at wedding celebrations. Otherwise, the main use of flowers as decoration

The Roman mosaic below depicts one of the earliest flower arrangements known. In the 14th century painting opposite, lilies symbolize the Virgin.

was for garlands and wreaths. Wreaths of forget-me-nots and buttercups decorated ancient Egyptian heads, whereas the Greeks favoured aromatic herbs such as myrtle, saffron, laurel, sage, thyme and marjoram. Fragrant flowers were woven together, combining narcissi and roses, anemones and lilies, and particularly violets—to be worn on all festive occasions. Homer lists 63 known varieties of flowers.

Republican Romans particularly loved roses. They wore them as crowns, gave them as signs of honour, and as symbols of love and feasting. They used them lavishly for house and table decoration. Roses were eaten, worn, slept upon, and walked across. They were also used for perfumes. A second century mosaic (see previous page) shows a basket filled with roses, an anemone, carnations and what appear to be tulips.

With the decline of Rome and the rise of Christianity, the rose and another flower, the lily, assume (or perhaps change) their special significance. Paintings of the Annunciation regularly include a lily as early as Byzantine times. The lily is a symbol of fertility and chastity, representative of the Immaculate Conception. The rose, earlier a symbol of Venus, was translated easily to become the flower of the Virgin Mary.

In the latter part of the sixth century, Saint Radegunda invited the poet Fortunatus to visit her and he found the tablecloth strewn with roses, the dishes wreathed, and rosy garlands decorating the walls of the refectory. This was a remarkable event, for although roses were grown extensively by Benedictine monasteries, they were not grown for their decorative qualities but because they were an essential ingredient in most medicaments.

Flowers were rarely grown for pleasure in the Middle Ages and opportunities for creative floral decoration, we may assume, were limited. A few flowers may have been picked and brought home, but more as a random thought than a planned exercise.

By the fourteenth century both Paris and Rouen boasted considerable rose gardens and roses were used sometimes to decorate rooms and tables, and for chaplets; but probably no formal arrangements other than wreaths were employed.

Left: details from a 15th century picture by Crivelli illustrating a simplicity of flower decoration that has much in common with modern informal styles.
Below: a Renaissance garden, with roses, irises, lilies and other flowers; all have religious significance but also depict the contemporary love of gardens.

The Renaissance

The Renaissance was a flowering in all senses. Gardens again became places of pleasure and the Villa Quaracchi, in 1459, featured terracotta tubs filled with flowers. At this time, botany also came under the Renaissance influence and blossomed into a practical science with wide implications, not only for agriculture, but for horticulture too, since new plants were introduced from other lands. Beauty was becoming important again, stimulating a passion for flowers.

Still allowing for the significance of flowers depicted in religious art, the end of the fifteenth and the beginning of the sixteenth centuries have left us several paintings in which flower arrangements feature as details. It cannot be said that any principles of arrangement can be distinguished, but

roses feature prominently, as do lilies, the pretty seven stalks of columbine representing the seven gifts of the Holy Spirit, irises and violets. They are placed in little vases, bulbous and usually with handles, or in urns and other containers of great magnificence. Natural greenery is not rejected: the great pink and white roses (*rosa alba*) of the Renaissance shine against the glossy dark leaves.

The 17th Century

In *Flowers Through The Ages*, Gabriele Tergit refers to extraordinary vases owned by Madame de Rambouillet: 'There were vases with perforated lids which lifted up, with the flowers, when the water had to be changed.' These sound remarkably like the elaborate vases shown in a seventeenth century Italian publication. One vase (see over-leaf) has a series of tiers and an ingenious 'waterfall' arrangement to prevent water flowing out of the perforations in each tier. From such illustrations it

is clear that flower arranging had achieved some sort of status as an art, even though it might involve simply sticking flower stems through a series of regular holes in a container. Every flower was equally important and was given its due. These vases, and the numbers of flowers required to fill them, were not popular everyday items. Only the rich would be able to afford to buy them and keep them stocked.

It is tempting to look at flower paintings of the early seventeenth century, and later, in an attempt to analyze typical arrangements of the day. Allowance must be made for artistic licence. Flowers of all seasons are casually mixed together for a variety of motives—sometimes for the sake of colour tones and contrasts, perhaps also because of the

Below: this profuse 17th century display built along the hypotenuse of a triangle marks a radical departure from earlier naturalism. The version opposite is equally opulent, but has a more casual, if planned, style.

difficulties involved in painting such ephemeral subjects. But, clearly, considerations of form and symbolism outweigh realism. The large, massed bouquets are often accompanied by natural objects strewn round the base of the vases—snails crawl slowly past, birds' nests (complete with eggs) teeter precariously on the edge of marble slabs, butterflies perch or flutter, fruit lies lavishly strewn around, cut open or massed in careless profusion. Even the containers are objects of suspicion: artists like to show what they can do and painting flower stems seen through water in clear glass vases presents a fascinating technical challenge, but it does not mean that glass vases were popular. This point must apply to the arrangements generally.

Nevertheless, these works of art, particularly the canvases of the great Dutch and Flemish flower painters—Breughel, Verendael, Steen, Van Huysum and others—are there to be taken as inspiration for latter-day arrangements as well as to be looked at and enjoyed. From the paintings it is clear that flower arranging—though not perhaps as depicted —was an important aspect of the upper class social life of the period. We do not know exactly what arrangements were made for domestic settings, since written descriptions are rare. One suggests that baskets, grounded with myrtle, be decorated with flowers stuck through the woven sides— things had not, evidently, changed much since the second century, when baskets were still favourite vessels. Advice is given about tying bouquets with all the flowers turning out in a regular series of diminishing circles, the most important flower at the top. This is still the traditional posy arrangement today.

The perforated pots described earlier, of course, lent themselves only to rather static arrangements of flowers cut to equal lengths, and very likely only the heads of the flowers would have shown, massed together in tiers. The Dutch and Flemish masters progressed from this: their compositions, although balanced, are more carefree; foliage swirls and flower heads nod at the end of long or short stems; a certain careless, spontaneous formality results. The effects are rich, full and intensely colourful, but exact reconstructions tend by contrast to look hectic and over-bright. Art is one thing, life quite another; the charm of the flower

The cutaway drawing of an elaborate 17th century vase shows how the flowers could be arranged in separate tiers. The flower painting opposite is by the best-known of all flower painters, Jan van Huysum. It is typical of the time in its massed profusion of blooms from different seasons, grand terracotta vase and use of fruit and natural fauna for balance and symbolism.

painters is precisely that they do not faithfully represent, in all its gaudy detail, exactly what is in front of them. But as sources of inspiration, these paintings, in their choice of colours and massive mixtures of different flowers and foliage, have had —and still have—considerable impact on flower arranging styles.

The court of the Sun King, Louis XIV, at Versailles probably brought the incipient art of flower arrangement to some sort of apogee of splendour. Le Nôtre, the greatest gardener of his age, designed the gardens of Versailles and flowers disappeared from outdoors: instead, formal parterres, shrubs, arrangements of coloured sand, and even artificial flowers, were laid down. Roses, lilies, hyacinths, narcissi, heliotrope, jasmine and carnations were 'forced' for the spectacular flower arrangements inside the palace. Not only flowers, but trimmed hedges and orange trees in silver buckets decorated ballrooms and the mirror gallery. Again, paintings of the period show elaborate bouquets composed of hothouse plants massed together in bowls, urns, baskets and vases of rococo elegance.

Floral Passions

In the seventeenth century there arose passions for particular flowers. This phenomenon was often caused by the introduction of a new species into European gardens from abroad, and such crazes continued into the nineteenth century.

The Dutch tulip craze of 1634–7 is well recorded by historians. Tulips were imported into Holland from Persia, and demand for them reached such a peak that bulbs were literally traded on the stock market. The obsession can be seen in flower paintings of the period, which nearly always feature the tulip—most particularly the striped *Tulipa clusiana.*

Less well-known, perhaps, is the fashion for hyacinths which developed in the late seventeenth century; and for peonies, camellias and dahlias in the early nineteenth century. The cultivation of the chrysanthemum began in 1838, though large blooms were available only from the 1920s. Orchids were still rare and therefore highly desirable in 1914, although *Cattleya*, the florists' staple, had been introduced in 1818 and 1819. The *Lilium regale* was brought from the borders of Tibet in 1910 and in 1830 the introduction of the

Left: a van Huysum picture showing a comparatively simple arrangement with a strong central focal point.
The other two examples show the same style—seemingly casual displays with large blooms creating a focal point in the lower foreground, as in many modern arrangements.

closed airtight glass case, the 'terrarium', resulted in a passion for growing tropical plants.

Artificial flowers have from time to time been popular and ways of preserving flowers have always been known. In 1919 the 'Makart bouquet', named after a flamboyant Austrian painter, was indispensable to any fashionable room. It consisted of grasses and peacock feathers, and many of them may still be cluttering up attics, gathering dust.

The 19th Century

From the beginning of the nineteenth century, flower arranging can be studied in much greater detail because by then most of the flowers available to us today could be obtained. There was an increasingly rich middle class with money to spend on outward appearances, and Victorian and Edwardian ladies—and their homes—were symbols of their husband's social position. Flower arranging was an occupation of leisured ladies: they could not scrub the floor, but they *could* do the flowers. (Among the poorer sections of society, however, a superstition existed until comparatively recently that it was 'unhealthy' to have certain flowers in the home.)

The Victorian passion for rules, regulations, principles and efficiency naturally extended to the art of floral arrangement. This was facilitated by the large numbers of publications devoted to home, hearth and fashion, and a sentimental attitude to the virtues. A series of principles from *Godey's Lady's Book* and the *St. Nicholas Magazine* include these points: avoid gaudy vases; use a round bowl or tall vase (a rather terrifying large conch or shell-shaped dish is recommended to be hung from a chandelier); do not crowd the flowers in tasteless bunches; do not put more than one or two varieties of flowers in the same vase; do not clash colours; love your flowers: 'By some subtle sense the dear things always detect their friends'.

In any consideration of Victorian flower arranging, the importance of epergnes must be noted. One account runs thus:

People had large centre-pieces of silver or porcelain, filled with flowers. These epergnes were the pride of the household and during the day they stood on the velvet cover of the

Christie's

Christie's

19th century arrangements often used few species, and in the mixed version above, note how each species is grouped together. A developing sense of naturalness is evident: the emphasis in all three pictures is on flowers rather than form or overall shape.

19

J. M. Dent & Sons

dining room tables. In the 1880s, the epergne was sometimes replaced by flowers, especially violets, scattered all over the table. Garlands of flowers surrounded the whole table. Flowers were put between the fruit in the fruit dishes. Geranium blooms with leaves of nasturtiums in small glasses were a popular table decoration . . It even happened that a hole was cut in the table for palms and fronds to grow through, to give the impression of tropical vegetation . . .

In 1883, in *The English Flower Garden*, William Robinson encouraged the idea that single flower arrangements should replace 'the old nosegay masses and the modern jumble'. The notion of simplicity resulted in arrangements of a dozen carnations and some fern, or twelve long-stemmed roses being placed in a tall, slim vase. Both are very familiar today. Even as early as 1883, Robinson was recommending the lessons that could be learned from the simplicity of Japanese forms of flower arranging, but Ikebana did not attain general popularity until it was helped along in 1910 by a general fad for all things Japanese. Certainly, the mood for simplicity was everywhere—in clothes, furnishings, modes of life. The cool, quiet beauty of Japanese living and its artefacts was almost bound to catch public attention, but as with so many fashions, only the superficial attraction was grasped, and the significance behind it, built up over centuries, was ignored.

The 20th Century

The name Constance Spry is possibly the only name of a flower arranger known to most people not associated with the art of flower arranging. She herself insisted on being referred to as a flower decorator, and her shop was called Flower Decorations to distinguish the work she did from ordinary floristry. Her first professional engagement, and public success, was a commission to arrange flowers in the window of Atkinson's, the London perfumers. The windows, and the arrangements

An arrangement by Constance Spry: Made in the 1950s, it clearly shows the influence of Dutch and Flemish flower painters.

decorating them, were immediately successful crowd stoppers, of compelling interest to passers-by. Her influences at this time were from two main sources. The first was the Dutch and Flemish flower painters whom she studied and from whom she learned her care over the choice of each flower to create the mass, line and opulence of her arrangements. The other great influence was Gertrude Jekyll, who published a book in 1907, called *Flower Decoration in the Home*. Gertrude Jekyll was an inspired and inspiring gardener, and it is to her talent and influence that we owe many of the fashions in today's gardens and many of the established precepts of arranging flowers. As a flower arranger, Gertrude Jekyll had things to teach Constance Spry: she stressed the value of complementary colours rather than contrasts, the use of foliage from however bizarre a source, and the use of crumpled chicken wire to hold flowers in position. Of Miss Jekyll's own arrangements, a contemporary said (with all possible respect) that Gertrude Jekyll knew all about flower arrangement except how to do it.

Constance Spry knew by instinct what others painfully had to learn. Probably the most important thing about her was that she was open to fashion in the broadest sense. Everything was grist to her mill, and her 'innocence of eye' was able to spot possibilities where none had been perceived before by others.

Constance Spry had mixed feelings about the enthusiastic amateurs who started or joined floral art clubs. They wanted rules, which Constance Spry broke with impunity when necessary. Nobody can be a great, or even a good cook, simply by following a recipe. Nobody can be a talented flower arranger by ignoring instinct or not making the best use of accident. Far from setting flower arranging rules, Constance Spry was an innovator who set a style uniquely her own. It is not a style wholly favoured today, but that is the nature of fashion. She caught a wave of popular feeling for floral artistry at its peak and rode it for the rest of her life, from her birth in 1886 to her death in 1960.

Contemporary flower arranging has taken much from Constance Spry and much from the 'twelve carnations and some asparagus fern' approach. The result is two separate schools, and both are treated in detail further on in this book. The 'traditional' school, following along the path of Constance Spry and her immediate predecessors—and influenced to a degree by Ikebana—has developed specific guidelines for building both massed and linear arrangements, while the less structural, 'informal' school relies almost totally on instinct and colour sense in an attempt to create natural-looking arrangements in keeping with the relaxed style of modern interiors.

One of the best known informalists is the interior designer, David Hicks. He fills deep, square glass pots with tulips, the stems cut to equal lengths, so that the effect is not unlike a small 'field' of flower heads. He adapts the bouquet style by putting summer flowers by the handful into a bucket or ceramic pot, or makes a sculptural effect with a large spray of dried hogweed. In a sense, flower arranging has come full circle with the informalists; the emphasis is again on individual flowers and the importance of nature or the 'natural' in art: many informal flower arrangements are strongly reminiscent of the uncontrived styles of the early Renaissance.

Two arrangements by David Hicks: a single flower makes a composition in its own right; a mass of the same lilies, though more 'arranged', remains simple in effect.

Basic Principles

Ironically, the first rule of any art is that there are no rules. In flower arranging, no less than in any other decorative art, an intuitive rapport with the materials and an innate or acquired sense of form, proportion, and balance will combine to modify any hard and fast rules laid down for guidance at the beginning. Occasionally, an untutored genius will suddenly appear and create works of art as though divinely inspired—but for most of us, a capacity for spontaneous inspiration will only be fully developed through practice and experience. Even a genius will benefit from a proper training in his or her art.

It is fair to say that only when we know the rules can we afford to ignore them. By that time they will have become so firmly ingrained as to have become second nature. Our own very personal creativity will have been subtly educated so that the freshness of individuality is preserved, yet at the same time enriched, by an understanding of the materials and their capacity to be formed into a pleasing whole made up of a number of elements combined in a rhythmic form.

These elements, arranged together to form a whole, are: shape, colour, texture and appropriateness. And, whatever the style or size of the arrangement, its success depends upon the successful integration of these qualities.

Shape

The structure of a flower arrangement is basically a geometric form. Forms fall into two categories: massed 'bouquet' and linear. The linear form is

Below : a massed bouquet arrangement, subtly combining greens, purple and pink. Right : the severely vertical lines of gladioli are balanced by vesper roses.

Daphne Ramsbottom

derived from oriental flower arranging (Ikebana), massed form is traditionally European. Eight forms are commonly used: horizontal, vertical, diagonal, crescent, 'S' curve, triangle, circle, quadrilateral.

The horizontal, vertical and diagonal are linear forms. The crescent and the 'S' curve may be linear or massed. The triangle, circle and quadrilateral are massed forms. These eight geometric forms may be used singly or in combination to create the basic structures of arrangements.

Linear forms. In linear form, the lines of the arrangement must be clearly defined. Thus, the minimum of plant material is used and each flower, branch, leaf or other material is clearly seen. A creative use of space is an important element in linear design, and the effect is spare and restrained.

Massed forms. In massed 'bouquet' form, the outline of the arrangement is solid. Materials used are often not so individually important, and little or no empty space may be seen in the design. Few lines can be readily seen, and the final effect is dense and occasionally extravagant.

Method. The two methods of making both massed and linear arrangements, the 'traditional' way and the 'modern' way are explained in detail in chapter five (Everyday Flowers) and chapter six (Special Occasion Flowers) respectively.

Right: a triangular shape outlined by ferns and using dahlias, roses, rudbeckia and red hot pokers to add 'mass'.

Basic Shapes

Colour

Colour is entirely a matter of personal preference, and in this respect, more than in any other, rules are a limitation rather than an asset. However, there are one or two basic guiding principles of colour theory which may be useful at the beginning. Pure hues are those seen in the spectrum of a rainbow, but the colours of most plant material are lighter or darker variations of the pure hues of red, orange, yellow, green, blue, violet. Black, white and grey are known as neutrals, but white flowers almost invariably contain a tint of another colour. Flower arrangements are not often of one colour but it is often advisable to aim for a predominance of one.

For a beginner, the use of adjacent colours (see colour chart) will provide subtle and satisfying effects. For example, yellow and orange blend well, as do orange and red, red and violet, violet and blue, blue and green, green and yellow. Experi-

Left: the matt textures of the freesias, daffodil and narcissi point up the smooth glossy petals of the tulip.

ment with different shades of adjacent colours in order to discover combinations and juxtapositions you personally find pleasing. A practical test, of course, is to imagine any combination of colours as a colour scheme for a room or a dress. Look, too, at the colours of the flowers themselves—the rich, complementary colours of a pansy, the green and red of a holly branch, the warmth of multi-coloured stocks. All will give you inspiration to combine shades, hues, tints and tones.

Colour, of course, can also indicate temperature, and a cool profusion of blues and greens will create a quite different impression from the hot orange, red and yellow of another arrangement. Be careful about mixing hot and cool colours.

Texture

Visual texture is the result of light refracted from any surface. Therefore, a smooth surface will appear bright while a rough surface will look dull. Both, of course, have their own interest and their own use in arrangements. Colours are selected for

Pure hues are colours seen in the spectrum of the rainbow and, since flower colours are variations of these, it is useful to study permutations of colour and observe complementary and contrasting shades.

their relationship, but textures are chosen for their contrast.

Just as the dull white colour and texture of arum lilies glow against highly polished green leaves, so the rough outline and matt texture of *Rosa alba* contrast with the round smoothness of its leaves. Texture is abundant in nature and it is often helpful to a beginner to pick up leaves, dried seed heads, fir-cones, grasses, even fruit and vegetables, and try them out in combination. The smooth leaves of an artichoke will, perhaps, contrast with kale; grapes with a bloom could be placed with shiny apples; a downy peach with a nectarine. The dusky little flowers of a mimosa contrast with shiny buttercups or the trumpets and petals of daffodils. With rough leaves, use perhaps a branch of a sapling stripped to its smooth core; with a rough-barked branch, contrast smooth and glossy foliage. Gradually the eye is educated to appreciate possibilities where none seemed evident before.

Appropriateness

Just as important as shape, colour and texture is the purpose for which an arrangement is designed. In this respect, any arrangement is only appropriate insofar as it enhances the position or occasion for which it is intended.

When deciding on a flower arrangement, consider the colour scheme and design of the room, the 'personality' of the flowers themselves and, not least, the impression the finished design will give to the viewer. In an office, a simple bowl of daisies will look better on a desk than a spiral of orchids, whereas a large, elaborate bouquet will better suit the front hall of an office building than a bunch of wild flowers in a jug.

It is also important to consider the arrangement in relation to the point of view from which it will be seen. In general, flowers are not intended to be looked at from below. They should meet the eye naturally as it looks horizontally, or downwards. But from whatever view, shape, colour, texture and balance must all be combined through instinct and visual training, to produce a harmonious result.

Right: a massed 'mille-feuilles' arrangement of begonia heads by David Hicks combines richness and simplicity.

31

Selection and Care

All efforts at arranging fresh flowers will be to no avail if the rules for their selection and care are not observed, however adept the arranger, however good his or her sense of colour and design. There is nothing more disheartening than spending hours on an arrangement, only to find the following day that flowers and foliage have wilted.

It is most important to select blooms—whether from the garden, the florist's shop or the country hedgerow—in the peak of condition. It is also vital to curb impatience and allow the flowers some respite and refreshment before arranging them. And finally, a few minutes spent daily tending finished arrangements will prolong their lives and keep them looking fresh and crisp.

Cutting Garden Flowers

Gentle handling when cutting flowers will prevent plants from becoming disfigured and stunted, and cut blooms from being damaged and bruised. If you want to be kind both to the flowers selected for arrangements and to the plants on which they grow, it is important to understand that there is much more to gathering flowers in the garden than simply breaking the stems by hand and amassing a colourful bunch or basketful.

When to Pick

In warm weather the best time of day to pick flowers and foliage is in the evening, when plants contain maximum food reserves, accumulated during the hours of sunlight. A further advantage of cutting flowers in the evening is that they can be left to soak in water overnight, before being arranged in the morning.

Some experts prefer to cut flowers early in the morning when they are still turgid with dew and have been revived by the cool, damp night air.

Whichever time of day you choose—and there is much to be said for experiment—do not cut flowers at the height of the day when they are at their most debilitated and limp after losing water

Beautiful flower gardens are synonymous with earthly paradises. They also provide flower arrangers with abundant blooms and foliage for creative use indoors.

in the sun. If, however, the weather is wet and cloudy, then it is possible to pick flowers at any time of the day.

How to Pick

Basic principles. A plant consists of about nine-tenths water. Its main source of moisture is in the soil so, when a flower is cut its main water supply is removed and, since moisture in a stem keeps it turgid and rigid, the stem will quickly become limp. It is therefore most important when cutting flowers to do two things: first, cut the stem in such a way as to facilitate the absorption of as much water as possible; second, put cut stems into water immediately so that they are away from a water supply for as brief a time as possible.

Equipment. To make a clean cut when picking flowers, a pair of clippers for woody stalks and a pair of flower scissors with a serrated edge for softer stems are needed. This equipment is essential since you should never pull or break stems by hand as this bruises them and does not give a clean cut.

You will also need a bucket in which to put the cut stems as they are picked. It is possible to use an ordinary household bucket, but florists sell special deep buckets with two side handles and this is preferable to the usual central handle which can easily damage flower heads. (More details about equipment are given in chapter four.)

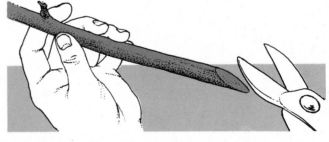

Angled cutting of stems facilitates water absorption.

Cutting. Ideally, stems should be cut at an angle (in the same way as roses are pruned) as this exposes the widest possible surface for the absorption of water. If stems are cut straight across, they tend to rest squarely on the bottom of the container and this reduces their ability to take up water. Although stems are generally re-cut during arranging and

some arrangers desire a 'squared off' effect which straight cutting produces, it is important always to cut flowers at an angle in the very beginning so that they can take up as much water as possible during their initial soaking.

Be careful, when cutting, not to endanger the future health of the parent plant. Always leave some leaves and flowers on perennials if you want them to live and to flower the following year.

It is best to bear in mind the colour, shape and height of flowers as you pick, with a view to the final arrangement. There is no point in picking so much at random that healthy flowers are discarded.

Try to pick flowers at the right stage of their development. If certain flowers are picked too early, they may not develop properly in water; if picked too late, they will not last long. As a rule, choose well-formed buds and pale yellow centres rather than fully developed, pollinated blooms.

Many spring-flowering trees and shrubs, such as fruit trees, forsythia, honeysuckle, lilac, magnolia and willow, can be picked with very tight buds. The warmth of the house (plus a little encouragement with boiling water; see Conditioning) will induce the buds to open.

Below is a chart giving the best times to pick some of the most common garden flowers.

Soaking. Flowers should be out of water for as short a time as possible. Put a bucket of water in a shady position in the garden so that flowers can be put in it as soon as they are cut.

They should in fact be allowed to soak after any special treatment they may require, as part of their conditioning (see opposite), for at least two hours. If you are in a hurry, however, and wish to arrange the flowers straight away, it is particularly important to plunge them into water immediately after cutting them so that they do not lose too much moisture. Use clean rainwater if you have a water butt. It will be necessary to take the chill off it in winter. Otherwise, use tap water, preferably with a water softener.

Arctotis	Firm centres.
Carnations	Tightly packed centres and firm outside petals.
Chrysanthemums	In full bloom. Tightly curled petals in the middle, and often a central dimple. Do not worry if outer petals droop.
Dahlias	Firm centre. Avoid large blooms as they do not last long in water.
Gladioli	Only the lower florets showing colour.
Hydrangeas	On new wood only; when buds are very tight.
Marguerites	Firm centres.
Michaelmas daisies	Firm centres.
Mimosa	The only flower which should be picked when fully developed and covered in pollen. It therefore does not last long and needs much care.
Peonies	As soon as petals open.
Poppies	Just as buds open and petals begin to show.
Roses	As soon as buds begin to open.
Scabious	Firm, light green centres.

Conditioning

Preparing flowers and foliage before arranging them is known as 'conditioning'. Some general guidelines are given here, and a chart of special treatments for particular flowers is given later.

The principles behind the conditioning process are the same as those applied when cutting flowers —to supply water and to facilitate its absorption. It is therefore vital to see that the severed stem ends are able to take up water. (Stems should already be cut at an angle, as described earlier.)

If it was not possible to put the stems straight into water, they should be re-cut to remove any seal or air bubble that may have formed. Cut at an angle, about 5cm (2in) from the first cut. It is best to do this under water to prevent air pockets.

Use flower scissors with a serrated edge to cut soft stems and a pair of clippers to cut woody stalks.

Stems should then be soaked up to their necks in deep, tepid water for at least two hours or, even better, overnight, in a cool shady place such as a garage or shed.

In addition to this basic treatment, however, certain stem types need special attention. If, before arranging, it is necessary to re-cut stems, any specialist treatment should be repeated.

Soft stems. These absorb water easily and need no further treatment. Some soft stems, such as those of spring bulbs, may become floppy if too full of water. It is therefore better to soak them for a while only, and to arrange them in shallow water.

Hard stems. These do not take up water very easily and it is advisable to expose some of the soft, inner tissue which will absorb water much more rapidly, either by crushing the ends lightly with a hammer or by making one or two 3cm (1in) upward slits in the stems with a sharp knife. (These techniques are shown below.) Chrysanthemums and roses are both hard-stemmed plants.

Woody stems. Certain flowering shrubs and trees, such as lilac and cherry, have a thick, woody bark which prevents water from being absorbed. It is helpful to scrape off about 5cm (2in) of this pro-

tective covering at the base of the stem before crushing or splitting, as for hard stems.

Hollow stems. Flowers with hollow stems, such as delphiniums, last longer if the stems are filled with water and plugged with cotton wool or tissue before being arranged. This can be done by holding the stems upside down and filling them under the tap, or with the aid of a narrow-spouted watering can or a small funnel.

Milky stems. Some flower stems 'bleed' when cut—that is, they exude a milky solution called latex. As it dries it hardens, forming a seal which prevents water from entering the stem. This process can be prevented by applying a flame to the stem ends until they are black and no longer sizzle, or by dipping them in boiling water for 30 seconds. Some experts also recommend pricking the stem just below the flower head with a pin to release any air. Then soak the stem in deep, tepid water as usual. Examples of flowers whose stems exude latex in this way are poppies (burning their stems is also said to prevent them fading), euphorbias, dahlias, tulips, and Christmas roses. Latex can harm the eyes, so do not rub your eyes after handling such flowers.

Crushing helps hard stems absorb water.

Expose inner tissue of woody stems.

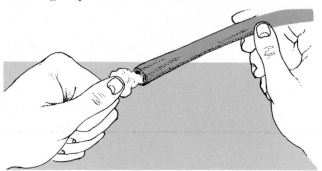

Plug water-filled hollow stems with cotton wool.

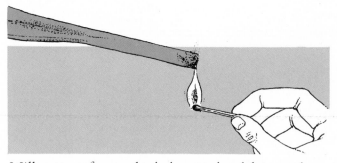

Milky stems often need to be burnt to break latex seal.

Bulbs such as daffodils, tulips and hyacinths cannot absorb water through the white parts of their stems. Cut them back to the green part and wash the sap away under the tap.

Water temperature. There is much controversy as to what temperature of water is best for soaking flower stems. Ice-cold water should never be used, and, in general, one cannot go far wrong in using tepid water every time.

It should be said, however, that warm water can be helpful, since it travels more quickly up the stems. Some flowers—chrysanthemums and carnations, for example—are reputed to enjoy a drink of warm water. Others, such as dahlias, peonies and stocks are even said to like fairly hot water.

The use of boiling water is sometimes helpful in sterilizing cut stem ends and preventing the loss of nutrients in flowers such as greenhouse roses and poppies. Dip 3cm (1in) of the stem in boiling water for up to a minute, and protect flowers and foliage from the hot steam with paper or a cloth.

To force open the buds of many spring-flowering trees and shrubs such as fruit trees (apple, cherry or pear), forsythia, honeysuckle, lilac, magnolia and willow, put them in tepid water, keep them in a warm room and spray daily.

Total immersion. Certain blooms such as hydrangeas and outdoor chrysanthemums last longer after being completely immersed in water for a few moments. Violets like to be floated on lukewarm water for an hour or so.

Foliage

Unlike most flowers, leaves can absorb water through direct immersion without any harm. Foliage which is to be used in an arrangement should therefore be soaked in tepid water for about two hours. Young foliage should only have a deep drink, but more mature leaves may be left overnight. The exception to this rule is grey foliage,

as the tiny 'hairs' which make it look grey will become waterlogged and will drip.

Excess foliage should be removed, not only for aesthetic reasons but also because it robs the stems of water. Certain short-lived flowers last longer if trimmed of all foliage. Three such flowers are lilac, philadelphus and clematis.

Leaves which will be under water in an arrangement should also be removed as they tend to decay, creating matter which clogs stems and makes the water smelly and unpleasant.

Grooming. Dirty foliage should be cleaned by swishing it in warm, soapy water or by wiping it with a wet tissue. Remove any damaged leaves. Ragged edges may be trimmed.

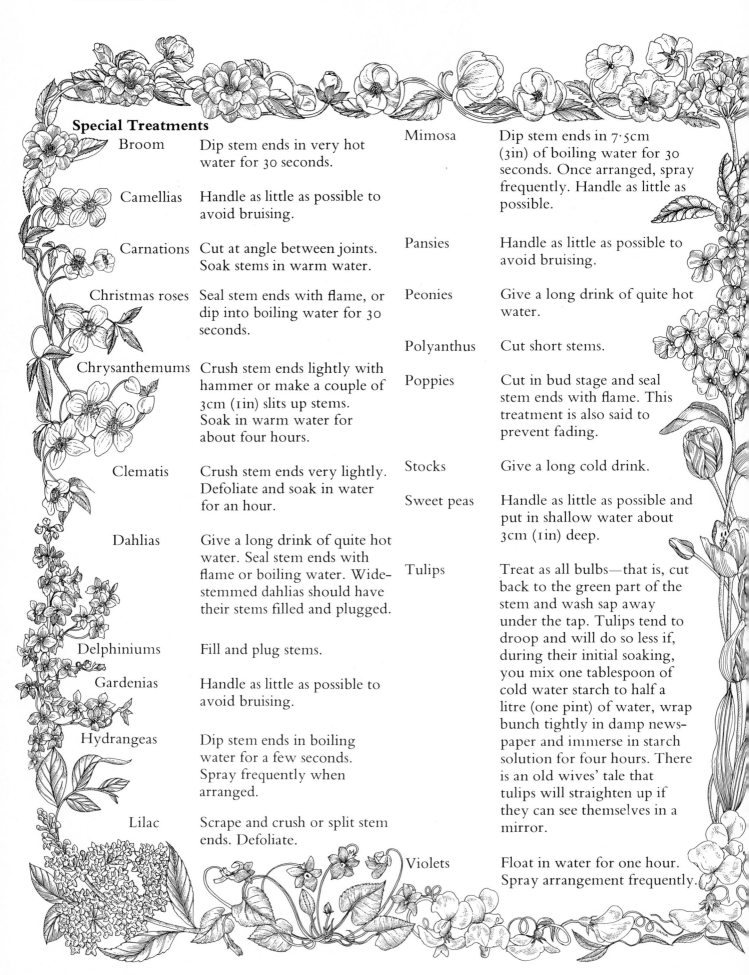

Special Treatments

Broom	Dip stem ends in very hot water for 30 seconds.
Camellias	Handle as little as possible to avoid bruising.
Carnations	Cut at angle between joints. Soak stems in warm water.
Christmas roses	Seal stem ends with flame, or dip into boiling water for 30 seconds.
Chrysanthemums	Crush stem ends lightly with hammer or make a couple of 3cm (1in) slits up stems. Soak in warm water for about four hours.
Clematis	Crush stem ends very lightly. Defoliate and soak in water for an hour.
Dahlias	Give a long drink of quite hot water. Seal stem ends with flame or boiling water. Wide-stemmed dahlias should have their stems filled and plugged.
Delphiniums	Fill and plug stems.
Gardenias	Handle as little as possible to avoid bruising.
Hydrangeas	Dip stem ends in boiling water for a few seconds. Spray frequently when arranged.
Lilac	Scrape and crush or split stem ends. Defoliate.

Mimosa	Dip stem ends in 7·5cm (3in) of boiling water for 30 seconds. Once arranged, spray frequently. Handle as little as possible.
Pansies	Handle as little as possible to avoid bruising.
Peonies	Give a long drink of quite hot water.
Polyanthus	Cut short stems.
Poppies	Cut in bud stage and seal stem ends with flame. This treatment is also said to prevent fading.
Stocks	Give a long cold drink.
Sweet peas	Handle as little as possible and put in shallow water about 3cm (1in) deep.
Tulips	Treat as all bulbs—that is, cut back to the green part of the stem and wash sap away under the tap. Tulips tend to droop and will do so less if, during their initial soaking, you mix one tablespoon of cold water starch to half a litre (one pint) of water, wrap bunch tightly in damp newspaper and immerse in starch solution for four hours. There is an old wives' tale that tulips will straighten up if they can see themselves in a mirror.
Violets	Float in water for one hour. Spray arrangement frequently.

Keeping Arrangements Fresh

Cutting and conditioning flowers and foliage correctly will ensure that they last as long as possible. But the care of cut plant material does not end there. The life of an arrangement can be prolonged if you bear certain vital points in mind both during and after arranging.

Make sure that all containers are scrupulously clean. Any organic residue from a previous arrangement will foul the water.

There are no firm rules about mixing different species of flowers, except that the sticky substance from such bulbs as narcissi is said to harm other flowers. It is foolish, however, to mix flowers with different lifespans, since it will obviously disturb your arrangement if you have to remove some wilted or dead flowers.

Aftercare

A few moments spent each day are all that is necessary to keep arrangements fresh.

A hot, dry atmosphere will encourage flowers and foliage to wilt. Avoid window-sills in direct sunlight, the top of the television (which is, in any case, potentially dangerous), a mantelpiece over a fire, the top of a radiator, the direct heat of a light, and draughts. Since central heating also encourages transpiration—that is, the loss of water vapour—it is a good idea to remove a valued arrangement to a cool place overnight.

Topping up. Add water daily. Some people recommend a complete change of water but this is not really necessary. It also disturbs arrangements and may cause flowers to suffer from over-handling. Flowers which quickly make water dirty, such as asters, marigolds and dahlias, and long-lasting flowers such as chrysanthemums, will benefit from a few drops of mild disinfectant in the water.

Spraying. Liberal spraying with a house plant spray will increase humidity and is particularly important in a dry atmosphere. Remove the arrangement to a kitchen or bathroom or outside if you risk damaging wallpaper or furniture.

Additives. There are some reliable proprietary preparations on the market for keeping water pure and prolonging the life of cut flowers. Some people

A few simple accessories help keep arrangements fresh.

add a copper coin, salt or sugar. One generally accepted method is to put a small piece of charcoal in the container to keep the water pure. Aspirin has recently been scientifically proved to be beneficial.

First aid. A wilted flower can often be revived. Remove it from the arrangement, or cut it off low down if removing it will disturb the arrangement. Then try one of the following methods:

Re-cut the stem (if not already cut) about 3cm (1in) from the end and soak in deep, tepid water for at least two hours in a cool, shady place.

Some flowers, such as roses, like to be floated on slightly warm water after re-cutting.

One easy method which sometimes works and does not require removing the offending flower is to put a plastic bag over the flower head to create a humidity chamber.

Florists' Flowers

How to choose. It is advisable, in general, to buy young flowers or buds. Look for crisp, green, unblemished leaves and perfectly formed flowers with light yellow centres. Choose a florist's shop which looks clean and well-cared for.

Flowers should be well-wrapped in paper with the blooms shielded from sun, wind or cold.

Conditioning. The cut-flower trade grows flowers that travel and last well. A good florist will have conditioned them in his shop. It should therefore not be necessary to do any more than re-cut the stems before arranging shop-bought flowers. If in doubt, there is certainly no harm in soaking them for an hour or two. If, however, you cannot get flowers home immediately after purchasing them, or if you have bought them from a stall where they have not been standing in water, condition them as you would garden flowers.

Wild Flowers

In general, the rules for cutting and conditioning wild flowers are exactly the same as for garden flowers. There are, however, one or two additional points to be made.

Picking. Above all, avoid picking rare and protected plants. If in any doubt, consult a guide to wild flowers. Pick with restraint; do not pick all the flowers from one clump, and only pick plants that are plentiful: *never* uproot them. Do not pick plants at all unless you can be sure of getting them home in a reasonable condition as it would simply be a waste.

Transporting. If possible, wild flowers, like garden flowers, should be placed immediately in water. This may not be practical, however. In that case, put small flowers in plastic bags and seal with elastic bands. Larger, woody stems can be wrapped in polythene, or in damp tissue or cotton wool and aluminium foil. Keep flowers out of the sun on the journey home. Once home, re-cut stems and condition as for garden flowers.

Flowers can be bought from road-side barrows or speciality shops but it is always important to choose a good florist who sells flowers in the peak of condition.

43

Materials and Containers
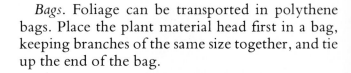

Before the business of arranging flowers can begin, it is important to have the proper equipment for cutting, transporting, preparing and supporting the plant material. It may seem tempting to 'make do' with a pair of scissors and a flower basket, but it is worth having the right utensils for the general well-being of the flowers.

Cutting Equipment

Florist's scissors, or stub scissors, have a serrated cutting edge which stops them crushing delicate stems as they cut. These scissors are also very tough and capable of cutting all but the thickest branches.

A sharp knife such as a kitchen knife is equally useful. In the preparation of plant material it can be employed to remove excess foliage, cut away knobs and shoots and to strip tough stems in order to increase their uptake of water (as described in chapter three).

Secateurs (clippers) are needed to cut heavy foliage.

Domestic scissors are constantly needed by a flower arranger for cutting tape and string, and for removing the brown, ragged edges of leaves.

Transport Equipment

Buckets. Many flower arrangers find they have to transport their flowers some distance by car, especially if they take part in competitions frequently. Flowers travel best in a bucket of water, and a wooden container can easily be made which will hold buckets steady in transit.

Boxes. Alternatively, a proper florist's box can be used to transport flowers. The blooms should be packed end to end in the professional manner.

Bags. Foliage can be transported in polythene bags. Place the plant material head first in a bag, keeping branches of the same size together, and tie up the end of the bag.

Other Equipment

A large sheet of polythene spread over the work surface makes clearing up afterwards a much simpler affair.

A small watering can with a long spout is a worthwhile investment for adding water to the completed arrangement, and is useful for subsequent topping up.

Successful flower arranging depends to a considerable degree on having the right 'tools of the trade'.

Stabilizing Equipment

Many arrangements need to be supported in some way, and the devices which are used to do this are referred to as 'the mechanics'. The kind of mechanics employed is largely a matter of individual preference but it also depends to some extent on the type of arrangement being made. Most flower arrangers use any or all of the following devices to support their plant material: a pinholder (needleholder), plastic foam, or wire netting (chicken wire).

Pinholders (needleholders)

Essentially, a pinholder or needleholder consists of a heavy base in which are embedded numerous, closely packed needles. Pinholders come in a variety of shapes and sizes, but you will find the most useful kind is round, with a heavy lead base and measuring 7·5cm (3in) across.

Pinholders are fairly expensive to buy but are well worth the money as they last indefinitely, if properly treated. Since they are easy to conceal, pinholders are especially suitable for shallow containers, or where a small amount of plant material is being used.

A pinholder (needleholder) can be purchased on its own or fitted permanently in a small 'well'.

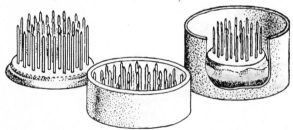

It is possible to buy small containers with a pinholder fitted in the bottom. This is called a well-type pinholder. It is not difficult to make one using a deep food tin from which the lid has been removed (it can be painted black to make it less obvious). Well-type pinholders can be concealed with foliage or driftwood and provide a very useful cheap container. They are particularly suitable for arrangements in a non-water-retaining container such as a wooden casket or a wicker basket.

Preparation. Pinholders, of course, require no preparation themselves, but the container may. If it is too deep, the pinholder may have to be built up on a false bottom as shown below.

To do this, fill the vase with fine sand or gravel to within 5cm (2in) of the rim, and place the pinholder on the top; add water until the pinholder is entirely covered. Bear in mind that the container must always be deep enough for water to stand above the top of the pins.

Anchorage. Even heavy-based pinholders may be inclined to shift around. Less experienced arrangers, particularly, may find it difficult to balance an arrangement and the pinholder will tend to topple. It can be held steady by sticking waterproof clay to the bottom of the pinholder. Special compounds are available for this purpose but children's modelling clay works just as well. Stick small knobs or a 'sausage' of the adhesive to the base of the pinholder, first making sure that both it and the container are absolutely dry.

In a deep container, a pinholder can be built up on a platform of sand or fine gravel. If a pinholder is to be in direct contact with the bottom of the container, it can be anchored with adhesive clay.

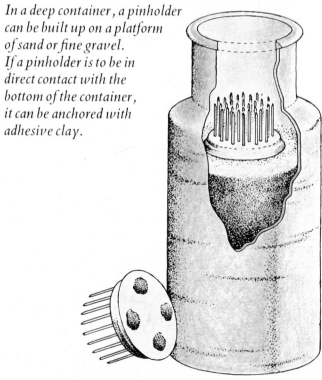

Press the pinholder down on the bottom of the container and twist it slightly to make the clay grip. The container and pinholder are then ready for immediate use.

Insertion. Press stems down on to the prongs of the pinholder. To make insertion of tough stems easier, cut the stem ends on a slant to give a larger area for the pins to penetrate.

Woody stems can be cut upwards from the bottom as deep as the length of the needles, making it easier to impale them.

When inserting stems at an angle, introduce them vertically, and then ease into position by exerting pressure at the stem base.

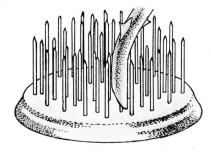

Introduce a stem vertically into the pinholder and ease it gently to the required angle.

Very fragile stems can be inserted into a larger hollow stem before being impaled on the pinholder. Alternatively, tie a small bunch of delicate flowers together with wool before insertion.

Pinholders can also be used to anchor wire netting (see section on wire netting).

Plastic foam

This is a specially manufactured substance, rather like a very dense sponge, into which the stems of flowers can be pushed for support. The best known brand is probably Oasis which is strongly favoured by professional arrangers and florists. Plastic foam will support almost any plant material with the exception of very fragile and very heavy stems, and it is the easiest to use of all the mechanics. However, it is expensive in the long run as the foam does not last but tends to break up with continued use. For this reason plastic foam is not perhaps the best buy for the beginner who may wish to remove and replace stems many times when learning the art of arranging.

Plastic foam is available in large blocks, in small rounds and enclosed in a plastic or wire framework to reinforce it. There is also a special brown foam on the market which is of a heavier consistency and is designed to support dried flower arrangements which, of course, do not require water.

Preparation. Plastic foam is dry when sold and it must be allowed to absorb water to its full capacity before use.

Place the foam in cold water deeper than itself and wait until it has sunk to the level of the water's surface. The length of time absorption takes will vary according to the size of the block and the brand of foam, but an hour is generally sufficient. The important thing is that there should be no air bubbles left in the foam when it is removed from the water.

Once foam has fully absorbed water, it must never be allowed to dry out again—if this happens, the foam will not take up water a second time. Therefore, to avoid loss of moisture when the foam is not in use, store it in an airtight plastic bag, tied at the top.

A block of foam may be cut either wet or dry to fit the container. Use an ordinary kitchen knife to do this.

Foam should extend to just above the rim of the vase so that stems can be inserted from the side. At the same time there should be enough space at the sides for more water to be added as the foam begins to dry out. (Foam should be replenished with water every day.) If the container is deep, build up the plastic foam on sand (see pinholder section) or put another block of foam underneath.

Plastic foam is available in rounds or in blocks and it can easily be cut with a knife to fit a container.

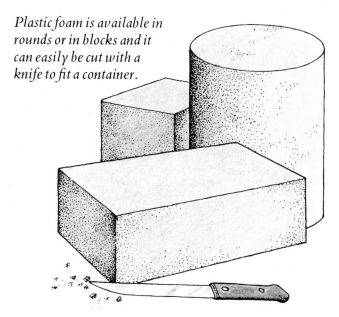

For small rounds of foam, and small blocks, special plastic saucers are available. These either have a built-in plastic circle or fitted prongs and are very useful for small arrangements such as table decorations.

To provide a specially strong mechanism, capable of supporting both delicate stems and heavy branches, place a cap of 3cm (1in) mesh wire netting over a block of foam and secure with fuse wire or string.

Anchorage. There are several ways to secure foam in the container.

A block of foam can be held in position with a special pinholder which has widely spaced needles. Do not use an ordinary pinholder as it will become clogged with foam. (To anchor the pinholder, see the previous section.)

Florist's arranging tape, a green, cloth-backed adhesive tape available in 12mm (½in) rolls, can be used to secure the foam to the container. (You may cut the tape in half down the centre to allow more arranging space.) Alternatively, use ordinary clear adhesive tape.

Insertion. Fragile flower stems cannot be pushed into the firm material of the plastic foam without being damaged. A hole must be made with a skewer before inserting the stem. Alternatively,

tie fragile flowers into a small bunch and scoop out a well in the foam to receive them.

Another possibility is to wire fragile stems before inserting them into plastic foam (see the section on wiring).

If an arrangement is to incorporate fruit, such as an apple or orange, plastic foam is the best base. Thrust three or more short pieces of dowel into the foam to form a shallow cradle in which a piece of fruit can be placed (see below).

A bunch of grapes can be made to cascade gracefully from an arrangement by anchoring the stem to the plastic foam with an ordinary hairpin. Simply pierce the stem of the bunch with one prong of the pin and then push the whole hairpin well down into the foam.

Candles can be decorated as follows: cut a small round of foam in half so that it is about 3cm (1in) deep, push the disc of foam down on the

Plastic foam may be anchored in a number of different ways. It is extremely versatile and easy to use.

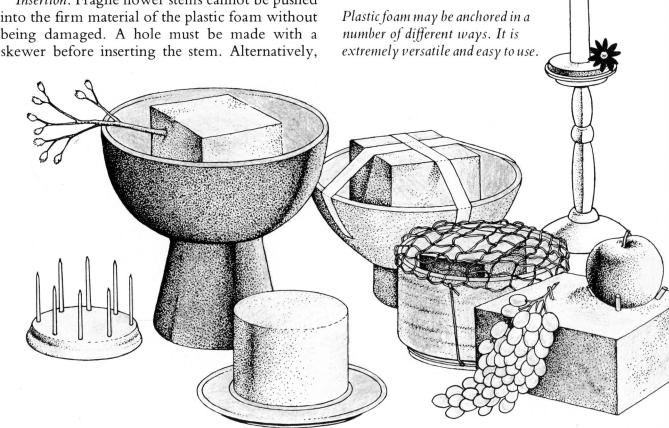

pointed end of the candle and thrust it down to the candle's base so that a coronet of flowers can be made just above the candlestick.

Plastic foam can be adapted for use in non-water-retaining containers such as a basket. Allow the foam to absorb water fully and then place it in a plastic bag. Tie the top of the bag tightly so that it is completely airtight and cut off any spare poly-thene. The foam can then be placed in the container and stems pushed through the plastic bag and into the foam. A skewer may be needed to make holes for the softer stems. Do not puncture the bag underneath or water will leak out and damage the container.

Chicken wire

Wire netting is not expensive to buy and can be purchased from florists or from an ironmonger. If it is to be used on its own, 5cm (2in) mesh is the best size. If the wire is to be used in conjunction with plastic foam (see the section on plastic foam), 3cm (1in) mesh is preferable as it will not cut into the soft material. In general, it is better to use galvanized wire than the green plastic-coated netting because the latter is rather rigid and difficult to crumple to fit a container. Its one advantage is that plastic-coated wire will not scratch and is therefore very suitable for use in a valuable vase or silver bowl. Do remember, though, that if plastic covered wire is cut in order to fit into a vase, exposed raw ends will be left and it will no longer be suitable for precious containers.

Preparation. It is important to use the right amount of wire for the size of the container; a good general rule is that a piece of netting should be as wide as the container and three times its depth. Obviously this should be varied according to the thickness and number of stems to be inserted.

Remove selvedge from the wire, using floral scissors. Crumple the wire into a loose bundle and push it down into the container so that the whole interior is filled. Any protruding raw ends can be wound round large stems for added support.

Properly fitted wire netting should extend slightly above the container's rim so that flowers can be inserted at a horizontal angle. Make sure there is a fair amount of space at the centre where most of the stems will converge. Do not crumple the wire too tightly or it will be more of a hindrance than a help.

Anchorage. Wire netting will tend to move around in the container unless it is anchored. To do this, place a pinholder (needleholder) beneath the wire on the bottom of the vase. Press down the crumpled netting on the pinholder using scissors or a knife. Use the first stem you insert to 'stake' the wire to the pinholder. The pinholder will also provide extra support for vertical stems in the arrangement. Rubber bands, string, silver wire or rolled adhesive tape can be placed round both the wire and the container and concealed with leaves.

Silver reel wire (see the section on wiring flowers) can be attached to the netting on one side, passed under the container (and round the stem if there is one) and then tied to the netting on the other side. Handles also make a useful anchorage.

Chicken wire can be secured with tape, string or wire, or by pressing it down on top of an ordinary pinholder.

Cones (tubes)

These are only suitable for large, massed arrangements. Cones are invaluable for making foliage more lofty, for lifting short-stemmed flowers higher in an arrangement and for making the most of heavy flowers such as lilies. Cones are green and made of tin and can be attached to a long stick with floral tape, as shown.

Put a small piece of wire netting in the cone to prevent stems slipping about in it. Push the end of the stick well down into the container and fill the cone with water. (Do this before continuing with the arrangement as it is difficult to add water to cones when you have finished.)

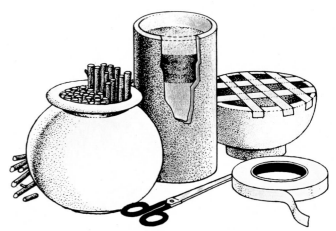

Simple, home-made devices for stabilizing arrangements.

In a tall, massed arrangement, cones (tubes) are very useful for giving height and prominence to heavy or short-stemmed blooms.

making sure there are no air bubbles trapped under the sand. Push the flower stems well into the sand. This is also suitable only for tough stems.

Tape. Make a network of clear sticky tape across the mouth of a vase. The container must be absolutely dry or the tape will not stick. Vary the size of the spaces in the network so that both large and small stems can be accommodated. This is a useful 'invisible' device for an arrangement in a glass container; the sticky tape can easily be concealed with foliage.

A narrow-necked vase or jug eliminates the need for any mechanics. As long as there are enough flowers to fit snugly into the mouth of the container, blooms can be positioned at varying heights and will be supported by the rim and by each other.

Wiring Flowers

Flowers should only be wired when absolutely necessary. Wire tends to make a flower look unnatural and certainly does not prolong its life. Many experts frown on the use of wire for any reason, but there are some instances where you will find it useful: supporting heavy flower heads and floppy stems; making false stems for fir-cones, heavy buds, and so on; for flowers which are to be carried or worn, such as bouquets, wreaths; and as stems for dried flowers.

There are two types of wire which are used for flowers: stub wire which is used to make false stems and reinforce weak stems, and silver reel wire which is much finer and used mostly for attaching flowers to false stems or frames.

Alternative stabilizers

The following simple and economic stabilizing devices will prove useful standbys for every flower arranger.

Several small twigs, cut shorter than the depth of the container and stripped of all foliage, will provide adequate support for an arrangement in a deep, wide-mouthed vase. This method is suitable for tough stems only.

Sand. Fill a deep vase to two thirds its depth with fine sand or gravel. Top up the vase with water,

Wiring

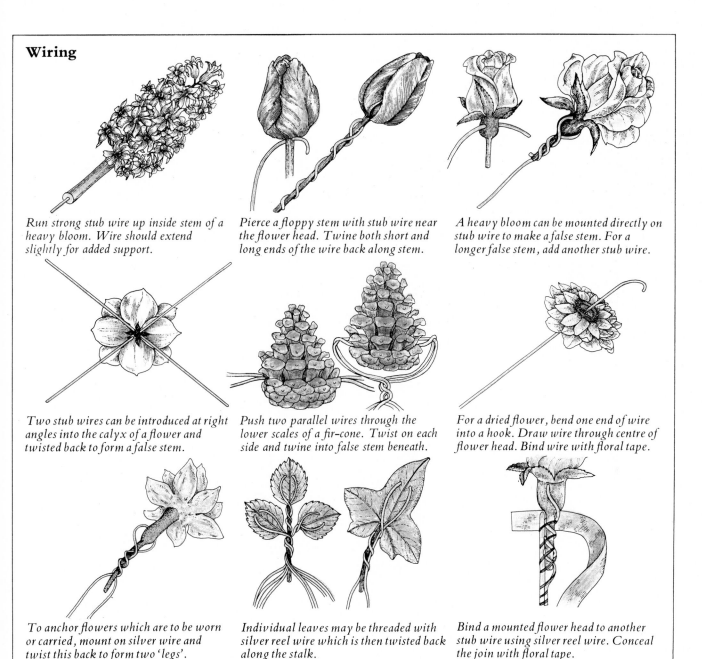

Run strong stub wire up inside stem of a heavy bloom. Wire should extend slightly for added support.

Pierce a floppy stem with stub wire near the flower head. Twine both short and long ends of the wire back along stem.

A heavy bloom can be mounted directly on stub wire to make a false stem. For a longer false stem, add another stub wire.

Two stub wires can be introduced at right angles into the calyx of a flower and twisted back to form a false stem.

Push two parallel wires through the lower scales of a fir-cone. Twist on each side and twine into false stem beneath.

For a dried flower, bend one end of wire into a hook. Draw wire through centre of flower head. Bind wire with floral tape.

To anchor flowers which are to be worn or carried, mount on silver wire and twist this back to form two 'legs'.

Individual leaves may be threaded with silver reel wire which is then twisted back along the stalk.

Bind a mounted flower head to another stub wire using silver reel wire. Conceal the join with floral tape.

Stub wires

Stub wires come in varying lengths from 18 to 46cm (7in to 18in) and have the appearance of long thin needles. The heaviest gauge is 1·25mm (18 gauge) but you will find a medium 0·90mm (20 gauge) and a light 0·71mm (22 gauge) useful as well. Use the lightest wire possible to support the weight of the flower. Stub wires may be bought in packets from florists' supply houses or, alternatively, a flower shop might sell a few wires.

Silver reel wire

This is very fine wire and can be bought in spools from floral supply houses, though fuse wire will work just as well. Silver wire is used mainly to prepare flowers for mounting on stub wire or on frames for wreaths.

Wired flower heads can be attached to stub wire using silver wire to bind them together. Floral tape or gutta percha, as it is called, can be wrapped round to conceal the join.

Driftwood

Driftwood is in a class by itself. As well as a means of camouflage, driftwood can be incorporated into an arrangement as a base, used as a container, or simply as a beautiful accessory. The term driftwood, as used in this book, refers to any piece of weathered wood—a root, piece of bark, the crosscut of a trunk, or a leafless branch.

Choose wood that will not require much re-shaping and will stand being scrubbed and brushed. Do not bother with a piece that is soft and rotting, as it will continue to deteriorate even after treatment.

Tools. A small pointed knife, wire brush (or sandpaper), scrubbing brush and secateurs (or handsaw) are needed.

Cleaning and preparation. Scrub the driftwood well in detergent and warm water. It is also a good idea to use some disinfectant and insecticide at this stage to purify the wood thoroughly. If you wish to retain the greyness in a piece of weathered wood, do not scrub too hard, but wash the wood gently.

Dry wood in the sunshine or in any warm place. Remove any soft, rotting wood from crevices with the point of a knife. Bark may also be removed if so desired, but it may require soaking in water for 24 hours before it can be easily dislodged.

Brush the driftwood all over with a wire brush (which may be purchased from any hardware shop); this will give the wood a natural, smooth finish. To give driftwood an additional silky smoothness, go over it with sandpaper, although this treatment does tend to destroy the natural texture of the wood and create a rather uninteresting effect. Grey wood should again be treated gently and brushed with a soft brush.

Re-shaping. Twigs can be easily removed with secateurs but, for any larger jobs, a handsaw will be needed. If possible, do any re-shaping out of doors or in a workshop, as it can be messy.

Shaping a base. To obtain a cutting line, dip the driftwood in a bucket of water, holding it at the angle you wish it to stand. It is then easy to cut along the tidemark with a saw and thus create a flat base. Alternatively, make a chalk line just above the water level and cut along that.

Colouring driftwood

Although the natural colour of driftwood is often sufficiently beautiful in itself, you may wish to enhance the wood with artificial colouring or obtain some special effect to complement a flower arrangement.

Bleached wood. Soak the wood in a bucket of water containing half a bottle of bleach. Do a section at a time, if the piece of wood is too large to fit into a bucket all at once—each part must be immersed in bleach overnight. A yellow, bleached look will be the result. Rinse and dry after bleaching.

For a pinker appearance, soak the wood for ten minutes in a solution of oxalic acid (1 tablespoon of crystals to 1·2 litres (2 pints) of water), then rinse with water.

Grey wood can be obtained by soaking the wood in a bucket of water in which 230gm ($\frac{1}{2}$lb) of salt has been dissolved. If possible, dry the wood in hot

sunshine as this assists the bleaching process. Repeat this treatment several times.

Stained wood. To make wood darker, use coloured shoe polish which both stains and polishes the wood. Test the colour first on a hidden corner of the driftwood.

Either linseed oil or wood stain will darken wood. Apply varnish over the stain for a shine.

Black wood can be obtained with a blow lamp, or by applying black matt paint or shoe polish.

Mottled or highlighted wood. To achieve a mottled effect, paint the wood and wipe some of the wet paint off again. Alternatively, paint the wood in three colours and rub the dried paint with steel wool so that the colours show through unevenly. A third possibility is to spray the wood with matt or shiny aerosol paint, leaving some of the wood showing through. Aerosol sprays can also be used to highlight driftwood in gold, silver or copper.

Polishing. Furniture wax or uncoloured shoe polish are both excellent for giving driftwood a gentle shine. Brush the wax on liberally and leave it for 24 hours. Brush again for a shine and finish with a soft cloth. Repeat for a stronger shine.

Varnishing. Use a colourless, matt varnish or the shine will look unnaturally hard. Varnish provides a complete protection from water.

N.B. Grey wood must be left unvarnished and unwaxed or the greyness will be lost.

Mechanics

A piece of wood can be made to stand on its own by making small permanent props (see opposite).

Drill a hole in the wood to the same diameter as a piece of dowel. The drilling must be made at such an angle that, when the dowel is inserted and cut to the right length, it will prop up the driftwood in the position you require. Cut the dowel *after* fitting it into the drilled hole, to avoid making mistakes. Glue the dowel in position, if necessary. Sometimes more than one 'peg leg' will be needed to support a piece of driftwood. For less obvious props, use small lengths of wood of the same type as the driftwood, or pieces cut from the original.

False legs. A piece of dowel can act as an extension, as well as a prop, to driftwood; a false leg gives extra support to branches, stems and roots and also lengthens them if necessary.

Attach a false leg as for props (see below), angled so that the driftwood will be in the required position when inserted in the mechanics of the arrangement. Short false legs can be inserted in a pinholder (more than one leg may be necessary). Longer legs may be pushed down into a block of plastic foam or into sand in a deep container.

Never attempt to push large branches into foam without attaching a false leg, as the foam will crack with the weight. Covered with a cap of wire netting, plastic foam is capable of supporting light branches.

A pinholder will hold fairly light branches and stems. It is sometimes helpful to split the stem end with secateurs, however, to make insertion of the branches easier.

Clamp. This is a special device for holding driftwood branches, stems or roots in position. The clamp will take fairly wide pieces of wood and is attached to an upside down pinholder.

The pinholder on the clamp is pushed firmly down on to an ordinary pinholder and the two groups of needles will lock together. A clamp is rather bulky and difficult to conceal.

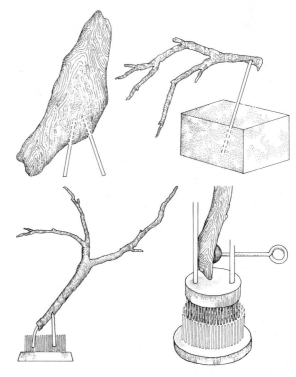

Driftwood can be supported with small props, a false leg or in a special clamp attached to an inverted pinholder.

Containers

At one time, all containers for flowers were called vases, and although they differed in design, shape and material, there was a strong similarity between them which imposed certain limitations on flower arrangers. However, in contemporary flower arranging the container may be any number of improvised items and it is seen as an integral part of the design, and not simply as something capable of holding water and stems. In fact, with products such as floral foam on the market, the container does not even have to hold water.

Essentials. Most people have several containers readily available, particularly as almost anything can be used, but when buying new containers it is worth knowing that the three most useful shapes are a tall narrow cylinder, a wide shallow bowl,

and a bowl shape on top of a stem.

Unusual containers. Apart from the obvious vase, bowl or jug—all of which still have a place in flower arranging—any of the following should be considered: a candlestick, with candle-cup fitted; a china or glass dish; a pie dish; any china or pottery container of any shape; a drinking glass or goblet; a brandy balloon, (especially for a single bloom); a casserole dish; a bottle; an empty tin can, painted or papered on the outside; a fruit bowl, either glass or wooden; a bread basket; a tea or coffee pot; and an egg cup for tiny posies.

Proportions. Because the container should contribute to the overall effect, it should neither overwhelm the plant material in it, nor be overwhelmed by it. The shape, size and height of the container in relation to the plant material are all very important.

As a general guide, it is said that plant material

should measure the height and width of the container, plus half as much again. But it is a mistake to be bound by this and it is probably better to trust the eye. For instance, if both the height and the width of the plant material conform to this 'ideal' measure it is likely to dwarf the container; conversely, if the container is very heavy or ornate, the plant material may need to be as much as twice or three times the measure. It is also worth remembering that the height and width of the plant material are not the only factors to be taken into consideration when judging proportion; the bulk, colour and density, which contribute to the visual weight, are also important.

Colour. Neutral colours such as those of earth, bark, bracken, stone and dark foliage show off most plant material to advantage. Bright colours, and especially white, are harder to in-

tegrate. But almost any colour can be integrated if one or two flowers of the same shade are added to provide the necessary link.

Position. The position to be occupied by the arrangement is one of the fundamental points to be taken into consideration when making an overall plan—and the overall plan must include the height, shape and colour of the container. As a very obvious example, an arrangement for a buffet which will be on a long, flat surface and will be viewed by people standing up should be a tall arrangement in a tall container, to add interest.

Although it is important to study the empty container before beginning, in order to assess its possibilities and limitations, it is never helpful to consider it in isolation. Its suitability will depend entirely upon the position it is to occupy, the plant material it is to bear, and the general effect required.

Everyday Flowers

This chapter is about flowers for everyday life, informal and natural-looking arrangements which become part of the general ambience of the house. Some will have been gathered in quick, spontaneous gestures, while others represent a careful choice of flowers and foliage. It is an essentially domestic matter in which flowers are complementary features, part of an overall decoration rather than 'floral confrontations' needed to furnish a barren area.

Since flowers are only part of the scheme, albeit an important one, they tend to be treated casually. This is also because the surroundings in which the flowers appear generally emphasize comfort and relaxation, and the flower arrangements must be compatible. To accomplish this, a new style has developed, independent of the conventional rules and in keeping with increasingly informal ways of life and interior decoration. This is known quite simply as the informal style and it is illustrated here by the work of two leading protagonists, designers David Hicks and Juliet Glynn Smith.

The Informal Style

The informal style of arranging emphasizes, above all else, a natural appearance. Flowers should look 'at ease' in their containers just as they do in their natural habitat. For this reason, informalists frown on the use of mechanics to support arrangements: pinholders and floral foam are too contrived; chicken wire is occasionally acceptable, but, as a rule, flowers should be supported by each other or by the lip of the container. If one or two droop, or fall outside the general geometric configuration, this is permissible for, as well as being natural, it can contribute to the relaxed atmosphere desirable in a room.

Undoubtedly, a sense of colour and a knowledge of how flowers behave are important in mastering this style of arranging, for the informal approach is very largely an intuitive one and inclined to the view that what looks right, is right. This makes it something of a hit-and-miss affair and, in the absence of firm ground rules, it presents a somewhat daunting prospect for the beginner.

However, it would be foolish to say that all the traditional rules of arranging are irrelevant. A knowledge of these (described in chapter six) can be very useful, and reading the rules of both the western and Japanese traditions will provide a stimulating background to the main aim of creating a reasonably natural-looking arrangement which is also a stable, cohesive structure relating to its immediate surroundings in shape, colour and texture.

Background

The casual or loose arrangement of flowers is not a new phenomenon, as paintings of the Renaissance illustrate. Although the choice of flowers is symbolic and they are usually placed in architectural surroundings rather than in interiors, these arrangements have an easy, unmannered simplicity about them which is very much in keeping with current fashion and can be instructive to arrangers at all levels of experience.

The flower paintings of the Dutch and Flemish schools are also worth studying for their choice of colours, their massive informal groups and the general relationship of the arrangements to nearby objects. But the balancing of an asymmetrical composition of flowers can rarely be achieved except on canvas. In a picture, fallen petals, a pattern on a cloth or other objects may counter an imbalance in the arrangement whereas, in reality, it is more difficult to balance a vase of flowers with another object.

Another painter whose work is particularly relevant is Matisse, an early, if unwitting, practitioner of the informal school. The correlation of a simple vase of flowers and the colours and textures of a room is one of his central preoccupations, and the flowers-in-décor theme is often carried over to a profusion of floral wallpapers and furnishing fabrics, until he has completely blended the flowers and the room (see overleaf).

A mass of peonies, lilies and sweet peas in a galvanized bucket is typical of the informal modern approach to flower arranging which is characteristic of David Hicks. Overleaf: anemones painted by Matisse in 1924 are an early example of casually arranged flowers. The correlation of flowers and décor is a dominant theme and of special interest, therefore, to flower arrangers.

How To Do It

Simplicity and naturalism are the keys to the informal style. Aids for supporting flowers are not needed although, in big bowls, large-meshed chicken wire may occasionally be used.

Flowers. The choice of flowers and foliage is of paramount importance. Whether the choice is made from a well-stocked garden or a florist's, there is always an element of luck in the availability of flowers (and in their arrangement), but flowers in season are to be preferred and, on the whole, arrangements should not include a great number of different types of flower. A single flower—or one type of flower—can make a successful arrangement, and too diffuse a bowl becomes merely a mixed bunch in which individual flowers get overlooked and their impact is lost.

Wild flowers, despite their fragility, are popular with informalists, as are all-green arrangements. Naturalism is encouraged by grouping the particular varieties as you might have picked them or put them in a basket, not by dotting the colour around the arrangement.

Positioning. There are two ways to arrange flowers in a container: either singly or by the bunch, and the method chosen depends on the size and style of the arrangement and the type and 'behaviour' of the flowers used.

The 'bunch' method is done by cutting off stems to the same length on a handful of flowers and then putting them into the container all at once. Each patch of solid colour can be arranged in this way. The flowers in a bunch can be of the same or different lengths, for their relative heights can be determined in the hand before cutting. Since enough flowers must be used to support one another, many blooms may be needed—20 roses, for example, for a vase 20cm (6in) across.

An alternative method of arranging in bunches is to tie several flowers loosely together and then position the others round this bunch in the vase, giving an illusion of mass. This is particularly useful if you are short of flowers but, whichever method is used, you will find that with practice the flowers should settle into natural and seemingly uncontrived positions. Both techniques are illustrated opposite.

The single method of arranging speaks for itself. It is suitable for arrangements which contain few blooms or little plant material, or flowers which cannot be cut together—lilies, for instance. The flowers can be anchored by their own stems, provided there are enough of them, and in this case a straight-sided or narrow-necked vessel is preferable. Alternatively, sturdy branches or chicken wire may be used for support.

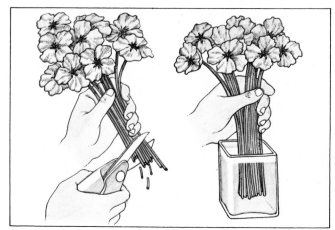

Arrange the bunch in one hand and cut stems evenly.

A tied bunch gives support to loose flowers.

Right: the mauve and deep purple of these two bunches of sweet peas are in daring contrast to the terracotta wall colour. Note the extreme informality of the flowers, obviously arranged in two handfuls with the lip of the vase as the sole support. The single stalk falling outside the general configuration draws attention to the overall shape of the bouquet and at the same time links it to the other objects on the mantelpiece.

Containers. Rules about containers may have been swept away (see page 56) but it is still generally understood that bare branches will look better in heavy crockery pots or in dull, possibly antique, metal containers than in beautiful, but formal, alabaster urns. Roses may look better in alabaster, but can also be put into pottery or baskets.

Arrangements without support obviously must rely to a greater extent on relatively tall or narrow containers. It is possible to obtain straight-sided containers made of glass, china or metal.

Glass containers can add greatly to the effect of an arrangement. Daffodils, closely packed into a straight-sided glass vase are a good example of this. If the flowers are bunched in the hand, and the stems slightly twisted as you put them into the water, the linear effect is a pattern in itself.

A rose in a specimen glass might have some foliage left on below water level, in order to add interest. If globular glass bottles are used as specimen glasses, they will allow a small amount of foliage to be seen under the water.

Flowers and Décor

Flowers are an enjoyable addition to every room. Indeed, one of the challenges of flower decoration is to discover how to use flowers in different rooms, and the same flowers in various ways in different settings. It is all-important that the décor of a particular room should influence the arrangement which is made for it, and the following points should therefore be borne in mind.

First, large arrangements are best suited to sitting rooms and hallways, as they tend to overpower most other rooms. More intimate arrangements will be needed for bedrooms.

An objective look at a room will pinpoint any 'dead' area that might need enlivening, or the best places to introduce colour. It is never a good idea to litter a room indiscriminately with pots: all vases should be part of an overall plan, some relating to the whole room, others to a particular small area, and judicious positioning can accentuate different features. This is what makes flowers an integral part of the interior rather than a predominantly eye-catching display.

Sitting rooms. Sitting and living rooms provide the setting for most flower arrangements done in the home. Therefore, they offer the best opportunities for exploring the introduction of new colour and for accenting the different features of the room, thus realizing its full decorative potential.

During times of normal human traffic there are a few favourite places for flowers—a side table, coffee table, chest or mantelpiece—and it is vital to try innovations in these locations, since force of habit will almost invariably create a routine approach to their floral decoration.

Use a container that you have not tried in that position before. Reassess the space and its surroundings—both the material objects and the colours and textures. In this way it is possible to break through the confines of habit and familiarity and—by trial and error—make new discoveries about flowers as well as interiors. However, always bear in mind that flowers can be used to draw attention to a room, as well as to distract attention from it.

Dining-rooms. Much has been written about the height of dining-room table arrangements. With a buffet there is no problem, but when the diners are seated at the table it is obviously important that they can see one another over any arrangement. Tall arrangements would be possible, however, if the diners sit along the length of the table and tall vases are placed at either end.

Colour is of course of major importance and can be spread by using two or three small vases instead of having a central one. Small upright vases might be appropriate for one evening, floating bowls or similarly shallow dishes mounted with flower heads for another. Open, preferably fragrant, roses are a favourite choice for summer. And with a garden it usually is possible to grow enough of one variety to use a single colour, or have the particular combinations of colours which are happiest with your tableware.

Instead of a series of small arrangements down the length of a table, you could give each guest his or her own personal pot of flowers. Tiny pots or glasses provide opportunities for using small and fascinating flowers which, because of their size, are not usually suitable for arrangements. Small mixed posies have great appeal but, if you are using an uncommon plant or one for which you have a particular regard, mix them sparingly. Three kinds of flower or foliage are probably right for most tiny containers.

Kitchens. As the kitchen assumes more and more the uses of a living-room, it becomes increasingly a good place for flowers. But they should be of the most casual sort. Earthenware and crockery containers are particularly suitable for kitchen arrangements, and shelves or tables—out of the way of work surfaces—are obvious locations. Wild flowers, dried grasses and herbal foliage all lend themselves naturally to kitchens.

Bathrooms are considerably cheered by flowers and plants. Since bathrooms tend to be steamy, however, choose only those kinds which will flourish in these conditions.

Armfuls of gypsophila in a cylindrical vase form the largest object on the table opposite, even bigger than the lamp. Yet the mass of tiny flowers have a lightness which makes the arrangement complement the objects around it, rather than dominate them.

Lighting

Whatever the room, lighting is important. Species such as tulips will rearrange themselves according to the source of natural light. Window-sills can be difficult positions for flowers unless their profile is their main attraction.

Table lamps tend to emphasize the delicate hues of flowers in arrangements placed beneath them, and now that there is a vogue for small adjustable spotlights and clamp lights, these can be used to highlight the flowers in a room, and to produce interesting variations of light and shade.

Lighting becomes crucial when flowers are arranged for a dinner table. In the evening, by candle-light, the relation between the flowers and the surface of the table is most important. Whether the table is of scrubbed deal or polished mahogany, or covered by damask or lace, many attractive effects can be achieved with a little forethought.

The relevance of an arrangement to the entire table setting is important, but the contrast of textures, and the reflection of the petals in a polished surface are subtleties likely to be noticed on a dining table. Here, after all, you have a captive audience.

Left : the frilly texture of sweet pea petals is particularly obvious beneath lamplight.

Below : only the lily buds are in direct light : their angularity is as precise as that of the wooden objects.

David Hicks

Bedroom Arrangements

Bedrooms are usually decorated in muted colours, and it is important that flowers should complement the décor. Certain practicalities must also be borne in mind: for example, the container must be placed so that it will not be knocked over in the dark. The gerbera (Transvaal daisies) above reflect these considerations.

Right: here the common foxglove is brought in from a wild garden to the absolute calm of an ice-blue bedroom; the spires, laden with green and cream bells, have been coaxed into position in a delicate porcelain vase and the erratically curving tips of the stems enliven the room without disturbing its equilibrium.

Bathroom Arrangements

David Hicks

Juliet Glynn Smith

Simple ideas bring colour to bathrooms.
Above: grasses and cereals culled from the fields brim over the enamelled vase. The bunches of grass are arranged as they have been picked—a bunch of one variety and then another. It is an arrangement of much boldness and ingenuity and one that gives each type of plant some prominence.

Left: two potted plants in a basket are an 'arrangement'. The leaves of the pelargonium with their parasol-like form are the most important part of the plant. They are the central body of colour and around them hover the delicate scarlet flowers and a medley of evocative patterning.

Far left: a jaunty composition showing an inventive use of bathroom shelving and tiny ornaments to display flowers. The picture shows clearly the relationship in height between flowers and their containers.

73

Table Arrangements

Juliet Glynn Smith

Summer decorations for heat and coolness.
Above: scarlet and sugar pink are not common companions, so this casual grouping of poppies and wild campion may come as a surprise. However, the brilliance of the poppy lends an intensity to the mauve pink so that the campion flowers diffuse the harsh brilliance of the scarlet and the gloss of the jug. An ostensibly bright red and white tablecloth becomes a muted background amid this galaxy.

Right: a series of small glassfuls of marguerites is a delightfully informal way of dressing the table. Excepting the cherry-dotted cloth, the emphasis is on white, green and yellow and carried out in the choice of both daisy and first course. Both these displays by Juliet Glynn Smith are evocative of the countryside and demonstrate a fresh and simple approach to the ephemeral quality of flower decoration.

Kitchen Arrangements

Juliet Glynn Smith

The decoration of kitchens has become widespread only recently, in the wake of an era of antiseptic utility rooms. But as interest in cooking has grown, the kitchen has become an important centre of household activities—doubling as a diningroom and, sometimes, as a sitting room too.

Kitchen shelves and out-of-the-way surfaces are good places to put quickly created, casual flower arrangements. Wild flowers are particularly suited to kitchens where natural-looking surfaces, such as stoneware, basketry and wood, abound. Fresh herbs can also be used decoratively before they are prepared for the pot.

In the arrangement above, the tiny spiky flowers of wild euphorbia are echoed in the geometric patterning of the breadboard behind. The vibrant green leaves are combined with a brassica and scentless mayweed to complete this refreshing display of countryside plants.

Left : softly bristled Aaron's beard,
Hypericum calycinum, is used
mostly for ground cover and not usually
seen to such advantage as here, along
with the open faces of campion. This
happy colour combination is a much
neglected one.

Below : kitchen bouquet with a
distinctly nursery flavour : a bunch of
wild flowers that any child might
gather, given the right walk in the
right season. The taller wands are
rosebay, the others mayweed,
campion and brassica.

Sizes of Arrangements

Large arrangements have their place in every household, and might be used successfully in a bare corner, on a cold hearth or in a hallway. Wherever they are, there must be enough circulating space, and the container must be stable and able to hold enough water. If such arrangements are made by simply using branches bursting into leaf, or masses of green foliage, they will need less attention and last longer than a mass of midsummer flowers.

Such simple but imposing displays, also dried arrangements (see chapter eight), may be transformed for part of their lifespan by the addition of a few cut flowers. White blossoms such as white narcissi look attractive with largely bare, spring branches. A large-scale arrangement will provide the opportunity to use gracefully arching boughs such as Beauty Bush, *Kolkwitzia amabilis*, drooping branches of old-fashioned roses, lilac, trailing vines and clematis. This is also the best occasion to use an urn which should be placed high enough to show off the natural forms of the plants.

Floor arrangements in squat containers present an entirely different concept, and it is vital to decide whether they will be seen primarily by those standing or those sitting nearby. Viewed from above, a large arrangement demands special thought with regard to colour and texture: gradations of height and pendant or bell-like flowers, are virtually irrelevant and the interest shifts to contrasts made by flat-headed flowers or those with a delicate gauzy form. Viewed from the side, however, a floor container can make much of variations in height.

Medium and small arrangements are very versatile. The colours of the flowers and their containers can be used to complement an overall colour scheme, either with beautiful subtleties or with stunning contrasts. The possibilities of introducing new colour into a room are great, and flowers can be changed endlessly against the relative permanence of the wall and furniture coverings. Daring colour contrasts between decorations and arrangements, and within the arrangement itself, become easy,

Vivid pink and red in a pot pourri of carmine-pink and crimson roses, and scarlet pelargoniums.
Below: a small posy of old-fashioned roses, simply displayed in a glass tumbler.

once any initial inhibitions have been conquered. Bowls of wild flowers, and all-green or grey arrangements will help ring the changes.

Single flowers are the simplest 'arrangement' and afford the opportunity to cut an isolated, beautiful bloom or to buy an exotic, or out of season flower. Specimen glasses should be placed at eye level. If the wall behind it is not an appropriate background, a decorative tray leaned against it makes a good foil. A plain tray or one in an elaborate style such as eighteenth-century 'chinoiserie' will each produce

a different effect. A flower may also be added to a group of objects on a table, a desk top or similar miniature scene. It may provide a contrast of material or colour, add novelty to an old collection, or become an integral part of the group.

Natural-looking unsupported arrangements: a mass of fragrant Zepherine Drouin is shown below.
Right: a huge display of old fashioned and wild roses, peonies and alchemilla mollis, arranged in the modern style without mechanics—but using gloves.

Florists' Bouquets

Anybody who has ever received a gift of flowers from a florist will know how it can spell delight or dismay. There are those marvellous occasions when the selection is sheer delight and, perhaps with the exception of a few tiny blooms which would be best by themselves, all the flowers sit happily together. But occasionally one is faced with a bunch of ramrod carnations or chrysanthemums; all with long, long stems that have been cultivated, not for the home, but for the formal florist's display. There are few more dreary sights than a bunch of carnations pushed into a pot, all stem and drooping heads. But do not despair: hedgerows might provide wild carrot (Queen Anne's lace) or the fluffy seed heads of wild clematis (milkweed). Both look very pretty with carnations. Holly is another companion; substantial, glossy and green, it contrasts well in texture and colour.

Obviously, if you have a garden, you should have no problem with foliage. Even in winter you will have a good selection of green, grey and blue, and a variety of different leaf forms. If, however, the countryside is your only other access to plant material, the early part of the season can provide boughs of catkins or branches of buds or tiny new leaves, all of which go well with spring flowers. Later, at the other end of the season, the arresting shapes of bronzing horse chestnut leaves or oak leaves are very attractive with the ubiquitous spray chrysanthemums. Wild hips and berry-laden branches can work wonders for florists' roses.

But, if a trip to the countryside is not an immediate possibility, you may, during the colder months, use dried material such as pressed ferns, preserved leaves and seed heads.

If you are given a present of a dozen blooms, there are several arrangements that you can try. The most obvious of these is to pick the best of the blooms and treat it as a specimen, then make two or three other arrangements with or without additions. Roses without any extra foliage are probably happiest with short stems in small bowls, placed where their scent can be enjoyed.

A study in delicate hues: cream roses with yellow-green alchemilla mollis and simple candytuft.

Juliet Glynn Smith

Wild Plants

Wild flowers give us the chance to reintroduce into our lives a direct link with the passing seasons. Although their beauty is constant and their metamorphoses are a constant marvel, they arouse conflicting emotions: flowers from country lanes rarely last long once cut, adding a sense of the ephemeral, while stout branches, slowly bursting into leaf, provoke very different emotions. Unless you know the countryside very well, collection is unpredictable, full of surprising finds and sad omissions because of changeable weather, the lateness of the season or human vandalism.

Wild flowers are acceptable as decoration anywhere today. Just as basketwork became fashionable, so too have field flowers, and together they are frequently harmonious. Wild flowers can and do provide spectacular and wholly appropriate decoration for either church or country house, and this may contrast sharply with childhood memories of wilting flowers in jam jars. Wild flowers will last longer if they are treated properly, and this means picking them in the evening and giving them a long drink and an overnight stay in a cool place (see page 43 for details).

It has been traditional to arrange wild flowers in a loose, artless manner, but because of the fragility of their blooms, the colour is frequently lost. Bunching them can help considerably and, using this method, cereals and grasses can be grouped to make a much bolder and more interesting collection than if used individually. By contrast, the brilliant delicacy of nodding poppy heads is seen better if they are more loosely arranged.

Wild flowers have been looted, cultivated and propagated to fill endless herbaceous borders. In this way the wild pelargoniums of South Africa, the North American prairie flowers, coreopsis, gaillardia and phlox, and the verbascum from the Pocono mountains in Pennsylvania—all delicately wild in context—have been heightened, brightened and strengthened for use elsewhere. It is the delicacy of wild flowers, the poppies and the dog rose, cranesbill and daisies, that is so appealing and so transitory.

Two of the most useful wild plants for a short-term arrangement are cow parsley and wild carrot (Queen Anne's lace), and both of these go well with florists' carnations, as stated previously.

Trees. The seasonal aspect of the wild is nowhere more evident than in trees. They are useful for their young foliage before it matures to a dark green and is prey to wind and insects, and again in the Fall when the colours change. During colder months boughs can be brought in and 'forced', considerably anticipating the natural cycle.

Sycamores flower with beautiful greenish-yellow racemes and should be arranged so that the pendant flowers are seen to advantage. They also have green winged fruits, or keys. The flower and fruit of the lime is also beautiful indoors but, like the sycamore, will probably need some, or all, of the foliage removed.

Silky grey pussy willow and catkins of butternut and birch are other favourite trophies from the country. These should only be picked in the early stages of their development, long before they open up and are dusted with pollen. The early foliage of the whitebeam also deserves mention, along with the humble thorn bushes and the aristocrats among flowering woodland trees, the dogwoods.

Long before most of the hips, haws and berries have changed colour, the berries of the mountain ash are a brilliant red, and the fact that this occurs during the peak of the herbaceous flowering season is frequently overlooked.

Trees probably provide the richest source of enjoyment and interest of all wild plants. It is also true that those now growing untended in the country are by no means all indigenous. In searching for interesting foliage in the countryside, we are invariably indebted to the deliberate planting carried out by our ancestors. The spreading chestnut tree, for example, now an integral part of the English landscape and heritage, is a comparative newcomer, arriving only in the early seventeenth century. Once of equal importance in America it has now almost died out there, just as the elm is doing now in both countries.

Fruits. The Fall, with its subtle and vivid leaf colouring and the richness of its fruits, might claim to be the best time of year. It coincides with a slackening off of colour in many gardens and is the more welcome for the fruits it can offer. The berries may be black or red like the clusters of

various species of elder, ripening blackberries or single rose hips. Autumn is a time when much can be gathered from the hedgerows to be arranged alone or with late garden flowers, or preserved for the winter months.

Above: the sculptural quality of tall stalks of cow parsley can be seen to advantage in front of a window where the light shows up their angular stems and the delicate flat umbels of the flower heads. Cow parsley also looks good as a dried arrangement.

Foliage

Foliage is fascinating. Much of it is there the year round, providing the flower arranger with the means of creating interest, emphasizing a particular aspect of a flower, and relating it to its surroundings. So many people think of foliage only as a means of adding bulk to a few blossoms—as a few green leaves. In flower arrangements it has a positive role and its colour is rarely plain green. A brief look at some plants grown for their foliage will make their possibilities more apparent.

The smallest garden contains foliage on trees, shrubs, or perennial plants. The potential value of foliage for arrangements makes it exceptionally worthwhile to grow a number of different plants. The plants mentioned here are grown exclusively for their foliage.

In all but the best organized gardens, there is probably a limit to the range of flowers. But where there is only one rose bush in bloom it could have, in even the smallest garden, a bevy of partners. Perhaps this solitary bush is a deep pink rose with which a bluish eucalyptus is an admirable companion. The downy grey and white stems of *Senecio laxifolius* could also complement the softness of the petals.

A few broad green leaves of bergenia or hosta would look fresh with the roses, their broad surfaces would throw the flowers into relief, echoing old-fashioned posies. Colour contrasts could also be made with the ruddy leaves from a maple, or deepening harmonies with various bergenias; the coppery purple of *Cotinus coggygria*, or the more subtle, delicate foliage of another rose, *Rosa rubrifolia*. These are just a few examples, but clearly the matching of flower and foliage is of paramount importance.

Natural foliage. The natural look of some flowers with their own foliage should not be destroyed. This is always true of a flower in a specimen glass and of small spring flowers. Lilac leaves, for example, are uninteresting in themselves and are responsible for the fact that it is a dreary plant for most of the year. However, when using lilac blossom, it is unnecessary to add any other leaf because the lilac leaves, being small, emphasize the size and form of each bloom.

But often a change is a definite improvement. Some leaves can always be pruned away, or others added, if those attached have been eaten or damaged by the weather. There are some plants, like the chrysanthemum, whose leaves droop and wither before the flower, and whose submerged foliage fouls the water. In these instances the leaves are best removed.

By stripping some of the leaves from a stem a different view is introduced. This recalls how in spring and autumn the skeletal outline of the trees beneath a sprinkling of leaves is so much more interesting than a mass of solid green. Stripping or pruning is usually necessary when using trees and large shrubs. It also cuts out unnecessary bulk in the body of an arrangement.

Foliage arrangements. Some foliage arrangements can become semi-permanent: those of trees and ivies that have been properly prepared can last for weeks. Flower additions can be made either to the same pot or in a separate vase. It is usual to use fairly small-leaved plants such as beech or oak. Judicious pruning is usually essential to make the most of the natural form, and sometimes the leaves will need sponging and wiping with a little glycerine to restore their lustre.

All-green arrangements may sound at first as though they are exclusively leafy, whereas they invariably rely on decorative calyxes or yellow-green flowers. A few of these are mentioned here because they have enabled predominantly green arrangements to become established.

Alchemilla mollis, or lady's mantle, was a comparative rarity until recently. It has foaming heads of tiny acid-green flowers and very pretty leaves that are useful for many occasions.

Green tobacco is the very pale green version of the better-known white tobacco plant, nicotiana, itself frequently used with foliage. It is a tall and elegant annual of a gently angular shape whose flowers have a star-like appearance.

A softer green is found in the massed heads of the pale flowers of *Helleborus corsicus*. Its own tripartite spiked leaf is extremely effective and used to

Blue-green eucalyptus leaves overflowing a stoneware pot illustrate the inherent attractions and decorative potential of all-green arrangements.

advantage with blossoms of less distinctive contour. In complete contrast are the fragile disc-like forms of the unripe honesty seed pods. These are scarcely recognizable as the common papery element of so many dried arrangements.

Bells of Ireland, *Molucella laevis*, whose pale green calyxes are its attraction, and the euphorbias are among many more which are suitable, and which are quite different in form. Flowers with a slight mauve tinge, such as astrantia and some aquilegia, add subtlety while white flowers always make cool additions.

Leaf shapes can be used to structure an arrangement and relate the flower to the setting—either providing an angularity, as with *Phormium tenax*, or a firm palmate outline as is the case of *Fatsia japonica*. Delicate or frond-like foliage introduces a gentle softness in a geometric setting; acanthus leaves are a positive and timeless addition to an informal background. Heart shapes of trailing ivy leaves or long pieces of *Trifolium repens*, the ornamental clover, are excellent for small arrangements.

Also to be considered are the setting of the leaves on the branch, the orderly patterns that they make, or the attractions of a pendant habit. There are as many ways for leaves to be attached to branches as there are variations in shape and size. Amongst the stems or branches crowded with small leaves, the erect ivies should be remembered.

Texture. Many of the grey plants have soft felt-like foliage that makes them flattering companions for fragile summer flowers. They are at their best with pinks, red and white. The most velvety of these is the appropriately named lamb's ear, *Stachys lanata*. Another, the popular *Senecio laxifolius*, can be very beautiful in arrangements: its vigour and value out of doors almost belie the delicacy with which it can be used in the house. The stems and underside of the leaves are white and the leaves gently cupped.

Glossy leaves frequently belong to the evergreens—holly, ivy, aucuba. There are also fat, fleshy leaves characteristic of some bergenias; ribbed leaves typical of hostas, and the lacy tracery

For an outdoor luncheon, fresh strawberry leaves laid directly on the table make a spontaneous decoration and suggest lightness of mood.

of ferns. It is a rich field and all these mentioned are very common plants.

Colour is a predominant thought in discussions of foliage and it varies with the age of the plant and the season of the year. For example, the young foliage of *Pieris formosa* 'Forrestii' is a brilliant flame, making the plant look as though it were in bloom.

Frequently the underside of a leaf is a different colour from the upper surface, not merely a dulled version, and the leaves can be arranged back to front to take advantage of this fact. The use that

can be made of these two-coloured leaves will depend initially on the habit of the plant, the way it grows, and then on careful arrangement and lighting, as with *Senecio laxifolius*.

The natural cupping of leaves, their curves and folds, cast shadows that can be exploited, either by breaking up the colour or by making a pattern.

Bowls displaying a single type of flower.
Below: a double display of Rosa filipes 'Kiftsgate'.
Right: fragrant and showy philadelphus.

Plants for coloured foliage

The plants mentioned here are grown for their foliage. Many of them flower, but without distinction. There are also those which are noted for their flowers but which have leaves of value too. The magnificent Californian poppy, *Romneya coulteri*, with its deeply cut, blue-green leaves is one example; the evergreen choisya is another.

Green. The dark greens are to be found amongst the evergreens: *Mahonia japonica* with its yellow winter flowers, prostrate juniper, ivy, holly, aucuba and *Fatsia japonica*. *Elaegnus ebbingei* is a grey green; *Helianthus major* has large pinnate leaves of deep blue-green. The glossy, fragile *Nandina domestica* is a pale, fresh green, worked in a geometry of small leaflets.

Nearly everyone with a garden will have hostas, and among the green varieties is *Hosta plantaginea grandiflora* with slightly arched, glossy ribbed leaves. Bergenias also have good greens among their many varieties.

Variegated. There are so many trees and shrubs with variegated leaves that extra green and white, or cream, combinations are not always needed. However, leaves with a very bold colouring are those of *Hosta crispula*, which have a strongly marked white margin, and *Hosta undulata* with a green margin. Among those with boldly variegated leaves is the *Phormium tenax* 'Variegatum', a cream variant of New Zealand flax.

Among the dogwoods, *Cornus alba* 'Spaethii' has yellow margins to the leaves; *Cornus alba* 'Variegata' is green and white. Both of these have deep red branches in spring.

Elaeagnus pungens 'Maculata' is a popular evergreen with vivid acid yellow flashes on the leaves. It can be very useful in early spring, particularly in yellow arrangements with daffodils and forsythia. It is very gaudy, however, and on occasion some of the variegated hollies might be preferred.

Hollies and ivies must feature prominently in any selection of parti-coloured foliage. The ivies come in a wide number of white and creamy yellow patternings with pale margins, or pale centres.

An all-green arrangement of hosta leaves grouped with several objects, including a spiky onion head, which sets off the delicate green hues of leaves and surroundings.

David Hicks

Hedera helix Pittsburg is a bright green which turns copper. It is worth remembering the differences in size and shape among the ivies.

The main disadvantage of growing hollies is the time it takes them to grow enough to provide picking material, but, given that time, they are richly rewarding. There are a number with creamy white or gold margins, but one of the most attractive is *Ilex × altaclarensis* 'Lawsoniana', a hybrid whose bright leaves are yellow and two shades of green.

Gold. The most common—and probably the most maligned—of all gold plants is *Ligustrum ovalifolium* 'Aureo-marginatum', the golden privet. It has good long wands for cutting and can look extremely effective, especially towards the end of the year, arranged with berries such as the mop heads of black elderberries. It has a variegated leaf, but is included here for its predominantly gold appearance. New foliage is greener.

Another gold-leaved plant, making a small bush, is the *Lonicera nitida*, 'Baggesen's gold', which has very small leaves. *Philadelphus coronarius* 'Aureus' is also gold, or sometimes a yellow-green.

Blue-green. The most splendid, as well as the largest blue-leaved tree, is *Cedrus atlantica* 'glauca', with branches that sweep right down to the ground. Eucalypts, though not coniferous, are also evergreen, and there are several species, of which *Eucalyptus gunnii* is the most widely known outside Australia. The vertically hanging leaves have great appeal. The leaves of *Eucalyptus perriniana* encircle the shoots, gradually diminishing in size along the length, and they have an arresting and slightly comical appearance. It is the juvenile foliage of eucalyptus—shoots from pollarded rather than mature trees—that has the rounded form.

A very large, heart-shaped leaf of a glaucous blue is the *Hosta sieboldiana* 'Elegans', whose surface is patterned by ribs. However, despite its size, its magnificence—like the green variation *Hosta sieboldiana* 'Francis Williams'—makes it unsuitable for all but the largest arrangements. The smaller *Hosta tokudama* may be preferred.

The low, blue hummock of rue, *Ruta graveolens* 'Jackman's blue', has a soft lacy appearance created by the small wedge-shaped leaflets. It is used for small and medium-sized arrangements, and there is a blue-green and a cream variation.

Red-purple. *Rosa rubrifolia* is somewhat unusual, in that it is a rose grown for its foliage rather than its flowers. It has feathery foliage of a soft reddish purple and it is excellent as a delicate leaf that can be cut on fine long boughs. In autumn it has vivid, round, orange hips.

The rhus, *Cotinus coggygria*, is another graceful shrub with a scattering of oval leaves on long stalks and feathery flowers which have earned it the name of Chinese smoke tree. The purple variation is a dark coppery purple in colour.

Less well-known is the dark red-purple version of fennel, *Foeniculum vulgare*.

Among the other coppery variations of popular species are *Berberis thunbergii* 'Atropurpurea', and *Weigela florida* 'Foliis Purpureis', both of which provide long sprays, the berberis arching. The grape vine, *Vitis vinifera* 'Purpurea', whose foliage turns from red to a dark purple, has clusters of mouthwatering black grapes, which are, alas, only ornamental.

And, finally, there is an alpine version of purple phormium, *Phormium colensoi* 'Purpureum' which, being a smaller variety, is probably more versatile than the usual purple form of *Phormium tenax*, itself a handsome plant.

Silver-grey. The silver-greys are a very large group, but because many do not last well when cut, they do not provide as many candidates for cutting as might be expected. However, the greys are invaluable for providing subtle colouring and softly textured leaves.

Senecio laxifolius and the similar, less hardy *Senecio greyii* must be the kings by popular assent. Their appearance has been described on page 89 and only mention of the beautiful, very pale buds need be made. These burst into small vivid yellow daisies which are disliked by many, but are really rather pretty.

The palest of the greys is *Senecio cineraria* which has a number of variants, 'White Diamond' being one of the most popular. The leaves of *Senecio cineraria* 'Ramparts' are very lacy in appearance. Although these plants are often used the brightness

Spires of wild mignonette, combined with teazles and white campion, emphasize the curved clock frame.

of their colouring can be inhibiting. They can be used to great effect with delicate open sprays of hips from the climbing *Rosa filipes* 'Kiftsgate'.

The green-grey *Artemisia arborescens* is a tall, feathery plant which is a perfect foil for darker more substantial leaves.

Jerusalem sage, *Phlomis fruticosa*, is a very different plant. An evergreen, its leaves tend to look dirty when compared with the silver-greys, but the erect shoots have an almost sculptural quality with a formal leaf formation and leaves that are slightly folded. Tapering and initially erect, they flatten and bend back as they mature.

The small *Helichrysum petiolatum* is a gently trailing plant with heart-shaped leaves, much used in pots and window boxes. *Ballota pseudodictamnus* is also very effective. It trails with furry stems round which are cupped pairs of soft, small leaves. It has whorls on the stem with tiny mauve flowers, and some people prick these out with tweezers. Lastly, *Hedera helix* Glacier is a relatively small-leaved ivy, variegated with grey and silver. It has red stems.

Most grey-leaved plants like to live in full sun and tend to be duller and greener in appearance if they do not. But the *Elaeagnus macrophylla* flourishes in shade. It has long, evergreen leaves of a silvery grey-green.

There are some plants, such as the glaucous hosta, mentioned in the section on blue foliage, that might well be thought of with the soft greys.

Herbs as foliage

Traditional herbs embrace a wide variety of plants. Many of them, artemisias, for instance, are not normally thought of as herbs in the culinary sense. But even in the kitchen garden, the opportunities for foliage, or combinations of flowers and foliage, are still great.

The evergreen herbs, bay and rosemary, are among the largest of these plants. Substantial branches of both can be used with effect. Unclipped, the bay has a vigorous informal habit, its branches crowded with tough, green leaves. Rosemary offers long stems full of small leaf spikes. The emerging blue flowers which cluster along the branches are very pretty. Totally different use would be made of angelica and fennel, which have a sculptural quality. Their height, as well as their flowers and foliage are spectacular and both could be used in a vase on their own. The round flower heads of angelica appear as great fiery balls, unlike the angular fennel with which its own frond-like foliage is in excellent contrast. The comparatively rare purple version of this plant has already been mentioned.

Rue, another excellent plant mentioned in the section on blue foliage, has such a strong flavour that it has to be used sparingly in cooking.

Salvia officinalis, sage, is of rather more use in the kitchen, despite its powerful flavour. It is a most obliging border plant and comes in several distinct colours: dull sage green, yellow-green, purple and variegated with purple and pink. However, sage is not long-lived indoors and needs to be used with care because of the dull surfaces of the leaves.

Mints and thymes provide excellent aromatic patches of all different shapes and colours in the garden, but they are of scant decorative use because of their very strong smell. Tiny sprigs might find a place in a table setting using very small vases. This would be an occasion on which to use the flowering herbs such as camomile and borage, whose apparent fragility is reminiscent of the hedgerows. Pungency need not be a disadvantage on a table out of doors.

Parsley, the most common herb of all, has a dense bright green foliage which might be spared occasionally for small arrangements.

The Flower Arranger's Garden

The advantage that the owner of a garden has over his or her landless fellow is absolute, but the benefits to be reaped can vary surprisingly.

For all gardeners and flower arrangers there will be conflicts of interest between those flowers that are grown for picking and those that are not. Some, who have specific preferences for their arranging material, grow it as they might a row of beans, away from the flower garden, if too many identical plants do not fit happily in the pictorial scheme.

A design for outdoor entertaining: armfuls of white Baby's Breath make a simple statement of abundance and are displayed here in the most natural of décors.

The gardener's ambition to have something of interest throughout the year will serve the flower arranger well during the colder months when there will be interesting leaf colour and a succession of such plants as *Viburnum fragrans*, hellebores and *Garrya elliptica*, all bearing flowers. The use that can be made of walls, and such ploys as the staggering of bulbs, are all valued by the arranger. But even for the main flower season, planning and timing are essential and not always as well organized as for the winter months. Even then the flowering cycle will only become established over several years.

One of the most important things, when acquiring plants, is to see the particular variety that you want in fact, and not merely in a photograph. The colours vary so greatly that for their visual impact, size and habit, they need to be seen alive and when a new idea arises it is necessary to act quickly lest another cycle passes before it is accomplished.

Perhaps the greatest advantage that a garden gives the flower arranger is access to the natural forms of flowering shrubs, climbers and trailing plants. There are the sprawling, knotted, woody stems which florists' flowers lack and the rare and fragile flowers which are not stocked in shops.

Shrubs are permanent features in a garden yet it can be that very different plants, notably annuals or bulbs, combine to produce the greatest effects in an arrangement. Lilac, for instance, is marvellous with tulips of either the firm immaculate shape or the exotic 'parrot' varieties. But every few years bulbs have to be replaced. A different companion is the rather rarified tree peony, which has very fragile, open blooms that are also very beautiful with lilac.

Wall shrubs such as the blue Californian lilac, *Ceanothus integerrimus*, can be picked; among the numerous varieties of this species are those which flower in the early part of the season and which flower again later. It is rewarding to pay special attention to such plants which have, as it were, such added attractions as two flowerings. Especially good evergreen leaves, spectacular seed heads or berries, a perpetually flowering, climbing rose or

This floor arrangement of wild campion is achieved with the use of six discreetly hidden pots.

Juliet Glynn Smith

David Hicks

flowers that dry well such as anaphalis or sedums are well worth cultivating. Thistles, grasses and ferns are valuable both dead and alive.

The mixed bowl is a marvellous celebration of bounty that can be readily indulged in by those with gardens. But beware of the temptation to bring something of everything inside. Exercise restraint and choose very carefully, limiting the number of different species that are used. Some of the most successful mixed arrangements have no more than three or four different flowers or types of foliage. This should also be remembered in cases of simple two-colour schemes such as green and white or white and grey; the arrangements are for a home, not to be studied in a gallery.

Frequently, the juxtaposition of plants in the garden can provide inspiration for the arranger, and it is easy to walk around deciding what flower might go well with another—even to the extent of cutting something small and taking it to another bush to be certain of that choice. But usually it is necessary to fulfil the requirements of both house and garden by introducing plants in a garden whose sole purpose may be as a specific cutting material.

The colours and gradations of colour that can be grown are almost limitless: for instance, there are certain solid white flowers: lilac, phlox, *Achillea ptarmica*, chrysanthemum and the floribunda rose 'Iceberg', all of which are useful, the 'Iceberg' especially so. All are solid white and rely on the different petal shapes and general outline to provide different effects.

In contrast, there are many white flowers which include another colour, such as narcissi. *Carpenteria californica* has beautiful open white flowers with yellow stamens, and is a spring flowering evergreen superior to orange blossom. *Romneya coulteri* is a large poppy with a yellow centre, another native of California. White anemonies have inky black centres, apple blossom a pink blush, magnolia 'Williamsii', a crimson centre. All these could provide bowls of massed heads, branches of early blossom and arrangements of all sizes, and all could be used singly or in conjunction with other flowers or foliage.

Softly shaded peonies in a basket conjure opulence, sophistication and quietude.

Special Occasions

Special occasions cover a wide spectrum of out-of-the-ordinary events, ranging from a small dinner party at home to a church wedding or large reception in a hotel. At such times, flowers play an important part; they must echo the general mood and sometimes even create it. These circumstances provide excellent opportunities for the flower arranger to enlarge and expand a floral repertoire and to indulge in floral abundance and flights of fancy which are not normally possible at home.

A special occasion implies a certain formality and this applies also to the floral displays: they too must have a definite form or 'formality', and the methods used are therefore very different from those used to create the 'informal' arrangements described in the previous chapter.

All flower arrangements rely on overall shape, colour and texture for effect, but the more formal approach requires considerable forethought and planning. Flowers are not expected to fall into place with apparent artlessness. On the contrary, the overall shape must be chosen beforehand and the positioning of each bloom and piece of foliage must be carefully considered. An accomplished arranger can do this very quickly but a beginner will need to work slowly and must allow for a measure of error and dissatisfaction until the techniques, and their usage, become familiar. The flowers and foliage are the arranger's raw materials and success depends on his or her ability to compose them in an aesthetically pleasing way. A knowledge of flowercraft is an essential part of this ability.

Flowercraft. Art is about beauty, craft is about technique. The craft of flower arranging refers to the methods for making arrangements which have developed over many years. Just as painting has techniques for applying oils, developed over centuries and passed down as part of a tradition, so too flower arranging has methods which are a part of its tradition. A working knowledge of these techniques is essential not only to the creation of arrangements in traditional style but also as a useful background to all styles of flower arranging.

The bedrock of any art is its traditions and once the value of any new method is proved, it too becomes part of tradition. As a result, styles which are not traditional today, may be so tomorrow.

Traditional Style

Traditional arrangements need not necessarily be confined to parties, churches and floral competitions, but the informal atmosphere of many homes, the cost of flowers and the time and space involved in making such carefully composed displays mean that this style is less often feasible than a more improvised one.

As has been stated, traditional arrangements are the product not just of the individual arranger's taste but also of influences which have accumulated over generations. These include the flamboyant, massed bouquets which date from the 17th century, as well as some of the techniques of Japanese flower arranging. But modern flower arrangements in the traditional style are variations of these earlier modes, altered to suit the fashions of the day—and the current fashion is for less extravagant and considerably less rigid displays than were previously popular. Nowadays, for example, flowers are rarely wired in even the most formal work, except to make bouquets or garlands. Plant material is allowed, within reason, to do what it wants to do and, even in massive displays, foliage maintains its own spontaneous, gently sweeping lines. Overall form remains important, but not to the exclusion of natural considerations. Man's will does not have to overcome nature's in all instances.

Shape. The geometric shapes common to flower arrangements are illustrated on page 26. In traditional-style arrangements it is necessary to decide in advance what the overall shape is to be, and whether it is to be massed, linear or a combination of the two. One of the most popular shapes is the triangle, but variations of the circle are also common. A shape which is distinctively traditional is the Hogarth curve, based on the diagonal. It is described in detail further on.

Colour can be used in many ways. An arrangement can be made in one colour with foliage for contrast, or in different colours. In the latter case the predominant colour can be dotted throughout the display, or carried in a line through it.

A tapestry of country garden flowers arranged to complement the forest greens of a traditional wall tapestry.

How to do it

Traditional-style arrangements are usually made on a base of floral foam or chicken wire (details of use are described in chapter four). Flowers and foliage are arranged one piece at a time, and the three steps generally necessary to build the arrangement involve the creation of the outline, the establishment of focal interest and the positioning of filling material. These are shown below.

Outline. To make the overall shape, the outline is established first. Fine, long slender material (usually foliage) is fixed in the floral foam or chicken wire base at angles which mark the basic outline. In most cases the outline material is positioned so that it appears to come from a single point and subsequent stems seem to flow outward and upward as from a single stem. Three main outline pieces are normally used, but in rounded or 'domed' arrangements, the outline material borders the circular base and establishes the central point of the dome.

Focal interest in an arrangement is usually created by flowers whose size or colour give the display its dominant element—magnolia blossoms, for example, will provide a focal point because of the size of the blooms. Lilac can be massed to create a similar effect. The focal material is placed in the arrangement after the linear pattern has been established. Often it is centred in the lower foreground but it can also be placed in a pattern through the arrangement (see below). This must be done carefully, however, as it could produce a too rigid appearance.

Focal interest is sometimes used to emphasize a line, either vertical, horizontal or diagonal, which carries the eye through the arrangement.

Filling is usually added last. This may be flowers or leaves or berries, or any material that will lead the eye naturally from the strongest element, the focal material, to the points of the outline. It acts as a traditional 'in between' material to soften the design.

In traditional arrangements, outline is established first. Here miniature camellias and catkins (Garrya elliptica) are used.

Interest and filling is given by the addition of croton leaves which are pushed into the floral foam which is the base.

Freesias add colour to the outline, while the focal line is made with tulips and two daffodils placed at the front.

Massed arrangements

The first steps to creating a massed arrangement are to choose the plant material and determine the overall shape. At all stages of the work, the imagination and intuition are at least as important as the intellect.

Even in massed arrangements the shape is made up of lines and, as a rule, these should flow from the focal point to create a rhythmic, balanced design. It is necessary to decide what lines are needed to create the desired shape, including the height and width (a height of at least one and a half times that of the container is a safe scale).

As has been stated; focal interest must be established and one way is to put the important plant material at the centre. Working up from the focal point, material should be placed so that the eye is led up from the focus to the outline. The mass of the shape is created with filling material.

Linear arrangements

In a linear arrangement, three strong forms in three strongly opposing colours usually make up the design. A definite silhouette is an essential element in linear form and is accomplished by establishing a vertical, diagonal or horizontal line with outline material, perhaps a bare branch or a pair of bulrushes. There should be a transitional area with strongly distinctive material such as large, bold leaves, and finally the focus must be pinpointed, possibly with one or two vibrant flowers.

Space is important in linear design; it becomes a vital element in the completed arrangement. For example, a branch may curve naturally to form a semicircle. The semicircle may then be strengthened two-thirds of the way down by leaves, and the focal point of the design, its base, can be defined by a single flower. The curve of the branch will enclose an empty space which forms the fourth element in the design.

It is important to be restrained in the use of material for a linear design. Strength in a massed bouquet style comes from the extravagant use of materials, but strength in a linear arrangement is almost entirely due to what has been omitted, and the character of the few materials used. Delicacy is not achieved so much by the use of delicate materials, but by the slender line of the design.

Living Lamplight

Pale Magnolia grandiflora and cream gladioli lighten the darkness of an oak-beamed minstrel's gallery, and could have the same effect in a poorly lit hall or passageway, or a windowless landing.

The basic open star shape is formed with the stems of foliage, embedded in floral foam, and then filled in with large hosta leaves to give substance to the centre and to hide most of the foam. The tall gladioli are used to give height, but some of the magnolia blooms are placed low down to express their natural weight and make the focal point.

This is one case where the actual flowers of the arrangement have been used to hide most of the mechanics and to give bulk and shape, rather than purely to fill in and decorate.

Hogarth Curve

This is a classic design of the traditional style and one of the very few in which strict rules apply. It must always stand in a niche or against a wall. The perfect Hogarth curve is delicate, casual and elegant, and the lazy S, the symbol with which Hogarth signed his pictures, should be one continuous line. It must be arranged in a tall pedestal because half the arrangement falls below the rim of the container, and flowers must be anchored in floral foam because wire does not permit the essential curve. It is also important to use naturally curved material so that the line is graceful and not forced.

In the version shown on the opposite page, two suitably curved pieces of curry plant form the two halves of the S-shape, placed so that an imaginary vertical line drawn from the tip of the upper piece would touch the tip of the lower. These first two pieces of material are always the most difficult to place correctly. Once the curve is established, the rest of the material can be used to fill in and to follow the fixed lines.

When filling in, it is important to understand the correct proportions of the arrangement which, again, are laid down quite rigidly. The curve should be one and a half times the height of the container when measured in its entirety, and the width should never exceed a quarter of the length of the whole. Some of the larger flowers, in this case roses and daffodils, should be placed centrally to give the curve a focal point.

Because the tall container is such an integral part of the arrangement, it is vital that it is included in the floral colour scheme. Opposite, for example, not only do the green and grey leaves echo the shades of the onyx, but the gilt-bronze tone in the other leaves echoes the metallic tones of the gilt trim.

110

Daphne Ramsbottom

Reflections

An ornate mirror is half-encircled with flowers in a bedroom for a special guest. This design probably shows, more than any other, the freedom floral foam gives you to arrange flowers in unexpected places. A vase or container is not necessary when even the head of a cupid offers adequate anchorage.

Here, prepared floral foam is tied into a polythene bag, so that it will not drip, and the foam is firmly taped on to the cupid. Balance is obviously important, and it is necessary to get the main weight of the foam, and later of the plant material, central, so that it carries downwards and does not pull to one side or the other. The anchoring tape is carried across the back of the mirror for added security. The plant material is arranged in the usual way, except that the stems have to be pushed through the polythene as well as into the foam itself. If some of the stems used are not strong enough for this, a strong stem or twig can be used to make a hole for a more fragile one.

The colours used here are chosen to blend with the rose brocade wall paper in the ornate bedroom. The curve of the mirror is used as a guide and the flowers and leaves placed to complement it.

In the Round

Rounded arrangements are appropriate for a coffee or dinner-table setting where the flowers will be seen from all sides and where their height must be limited.

The domed form is built up by placing outline material round the perimeter of the bowl and at its centre to establish height. The rounded shape (below) can be created more conventionally, when the container demands.

On the right, the rich red of alstroemeria (Peruvian lilies) contrasts with the glowing berries of Hypericum patulum 'Hidcote' which form the outline of the circle. Floral foam is used to hold the flowers in place.

The lovely sunlit arrangement (left) illustrates how a container can help underline a theme. The blue and white bowl is just right for this mass of autumn flowers and has some of the luxuriance of a Dutch flower painting.

Receptions and Parties

Whether it is held in a private house, a hotel or a marquee in the garden, the atmosphere of a reception or party can be determined by the flowers, which may be formal or informal, light-hearted or solemn, meagre or opulent. The arrangements should be planned not only for their effect but for the positions they are to occupy. The size of an arrangement should be determined by the amount of space around it and the size of the room. For instance, the entrance hall of a large hotel needs quite a lavish display.

Hall designs

When planning an arrangement for a large hall–

Opposite and below: similar flowers are used in different ways for different positions in the same hall.

Left: seven metal tubes taped together and embedded in chicken wire form the mechanics of a tall arrangement. Below: a living plant taped to a tube with its roots in a polythene bag.

way, the two prime considerations are scale and shape. The overall shape should harmonize with the architecture of the setting, and the size of the design should be such that it is not dwarfed by its surroundings, but subtly enriches them. The different examples shown here can all be seen to conform to these requirements, each in its way.

Hall alcove. If a large arrangement, such as the one on the previous page, is created in an alcove, it is possible to let it lean slightly against the wall and in this way balance will not be the problem it might otherwise be. The mechanics in this display consist of crumpled wire netting in the neck of a tall container, which in turn supports a fairly elaborate structure of seven metal tubes, taped securely together, in an upward and staggered formation. These give support to the large whitebeam and copper beech branches, and both height and support to the more delicate pieces of plant material.

The whitebeam branches are placed first, both at the top and sides, to create the basic shape, followed by the copper beech branches, whose darker leaves give depth—especially important in an arrangement against a wall, which is essentially flat at the back.

The topmost branches, which are very long, are placed in the netting behind the tubes in order to leave the tubes free for the lighter material. Running out of space in the top tube is a continuing problem in arrangements which require height.

The arrangement was conceived as a pattern in pinks and greens, principally pink blooms and green leaves. To create variety and interest, and to form a link between the two colours, there are also the green blooms of mollucella and the pink leaves of caladium. The caladiums, visible in the centre and at the base of the arrangement, are in fact living plants. Each is tipped out of its pot and its roots thoroughly dampened and then tied up in a small polythene bag. The bag is tied firmly to the side of one of the metal tubes. The plants are among the first of the smaller items to be placed so that the later additions can be arranged to hide the bags. A plant will survive in this state for at least as long as cut foliage, and when the rest of the arrangement has died the plant can be returned to its pot.

After the branches and plants, the flowers are placed in such a way that they continue and fill out the shape, forming their own asymmetrical pattern.

When working on such a large arrangement it is important to step back frequently and view it as it will be seen by visitors. It is wise to keep a few blooms and pieces of greenery in reserve, in case any gaps need to be filled in.

Hall table. It is interesting to compare the hall arrangement on the previous page with the one shown in the alcove (also on the previous page). Because they appear in the same hall and must complement each other, both are made with the same plant material, but here the material has been built into an entirely different shape to suit its different position.

The arrangement's container is a round bowl filled with floral foam and wire netting, and bearing just two tubes to give a minimum of height and support. The background leaves are arranged into an open fan shape and the rest of the material is positioned in a low, wide spread rather than in the upward sweep which suited the alcove.

Corner display. Designed for a hotel hallway, the display opposite is made in the same way as the one in the alcove already described. The most important practical difference is that this one is free-standing and therefore balance is a problem, not only for the finished arrangement, but as plant material is added. While working on something of this size, it is essential to watch very closely for any signs that the container might tip. If it does fall, not only will the design be ruined but some of the plant material will almost certainly be damaged.

This is an autumn arrangement, but the potential bleakness of autumn is offset by the choice of hot orange rowan berries, gladioli and gerbera, 'cooled down' by creamy auratum lilies. Each piece of foliage is chosen for its good curve and general shape which make it possible to bring foliage and ivy down at the sides for balance.

Balance is a vital factor in the case of a large free-standing arrangement like the one opposite, and not just visual balance, but physical balance, too. If it is not absolutely stable the lightest passing touch will bring it crashing down. This display is made of auratum lilies, rowan berries, gladioli and gerbera.

Marquee Extravaganzas

Marquees are of such a fanciful, fleeting nature that it seems fitting that they should house equally ephemeral and fantastic floral displays.

Dance floor displays. A dance and a buffet in a marquee call for special effects, and the immense and seemingly casual arrangements shown here around a temporary dance floor are born out of careful thought and hard work. The mixture of local and exotic plants works particularly well because the designer is creating an environment which is neither indoors nor out of doors, but should ideally provide a link between the two.

The height and width of the arrangements are attained in the traditional manner, with the help of three tiers of tubes, but other traditions are broken, to good effect. Most of the outer lines fall downwards, and yet the effect is of lightness, happiness and gaiety, and the entire design creates a sense of flow and movement, as though the arrangement, with its trailing ivy and wafting grasses, is responding to the music as much as the guests themselves.

Buffet table. An arrangement for a buffet table should have height, partly to counteract the flat and potentially boring shape of the long tables, and partly because guests always view buffet tables from a standing position. In the case below, although the material is basically the same as that round the dance floor, which is illustrated opposite, real artichokes and peppers are wired in place to introduce the idea of food.

Flowers are a principal party decoration. The marquee opposite seems literally to be supported by a vast floral display (detail on left). The theme continues in the buffet display above.

Pour plaster of Paris into pot.   *Cover foam with wire netting.*   *Insert flowers, place in basket.*

Small tables. If small tables are not intended for a formal dinner or supper, but for the plates and glasses of people watching a dance rather than each other, it is permissible to provide relatively tall table decorations, whose height and general shape are in accord with the larger decorations around them. Such a decoration is the rose 'tree' shown opposite. The same idea could be exploited using dried flowers, or greenery (to make 'bay' trees).

Each miniature rose 'tree' is made quite simply with a smooth length of branch, or a broom handle, embedded in a pot with plaster of Paris; a ball of floral foam is then attached to the top. The foam is soaked first and encased in chicken wire to help keep its shape. The roses, alchemilla and rosemary sprigs are then pushed into the foam. The plaster of Paris is disguised with tufts of moss.

The rose is probably the most loved and most symbolic of all flowers. Arrangements of roses can vary from the single bloom, such as the one on the right, lodged in a crystal salt cellar, to the classic gift of a dozen roses simply displayed in a tall vase, or to more fanciful party decorations like the miniature rose 'tree' on the left. Roses have myriad shades and new species are continually appearing. Their fragrance is as captivating as their appearance and can be especially appreciated on a dining table.

Overleaf: celebration flowers, including roses, are arranged to cover a whole sideboard top.

Table Arrangements

The rules which govern dinner-table arrangements are dictated by common sense. A tall arrangement, like the cluster of sweet peas flowering from a silver candelabrum, is permissible so long as the guests are spaced sufficiently far apart to be able to converse around it.

Low, flat arrangements, like the orange roses shown overleaf, are easy to see over but should not extend so far that tendrils of ivy trail in the food.

Chunky arrangements, like the simple basket of blue flowers, should not be so large that they leave insufficient space on the table.

Before thinking about the flowers, it is vital to consider the table itself: how large it is; how many people are to sit down to dinner; where the place settings will fall; what else will be on the table; whether food will be served from a sideboard or put on the table; how much passing to and fro of dishes the meal will involve; and so on. In this way it is possible to see exactly how much space, and what shape of space, is available for flowers, and then to decide on the flowers and containers.

These three arrangements have been designed to suit specific dining tables, with size of dinner service and spacing of guests taken into account. Another example is shown overleaf. The commonest mistake is to spend time and effort on a beautiful creation which, in the end, is such a nuisance on the table that its attractions are lost in a general wave of irritation.

Church Flowers

The church has special needs when it comes to flower arrangements and—apart from the obvious courtesy of checking on the preference of the clergy, who will not appreciate decorations which impede their movements or those of the congregation, or which block sight-lines from altar to pews—there are three important practical considerations to bear in mind. Church lighting tends to be dim, and so flowers which are pale or light in colour will show up best. Most church arrangements are viewed from a distance, so intricate detail is a waste of time; the most effective arrangements are either those with clear, strong lines or else large masses or sweeps whose overall effect can be seen from some distance away. Finally, church flowers are generally changed once a week only, so that long-lasting material is essential. It is therefore very important to choose very fresh material and to prepare it carefully to avoid a sad, end-of-week wilt.

These general points apply to all churches but, while bearing them in mind, it is also essential to consider the particular church. A modern church will best be served by modern arrangements, an old church by traditional arrangements. Any specific points of beauty or interest should be high-lighted, never obliterated, by the flowers. Altar arrangements should be small and clear-cut, in keeping with the style and colour of the altar, and subsidiary in impact to the cross. The use of seasonal material is especially important; the church calendar guides the congregation through the year and the plant material must harmonize. This will ensure, too, that on special occasions the church is enhanced as it should be and that seasonal and traditional arrangements will appear on the appropriate occasions.

Altar flowers
Altar arrangements should be planned in pairs, although no two arrangements can ever be exactly the same. This does not matter, however, because the slight dissimilarities between the arrangements

These twin altar arrangements seem almost to draw the sunshine in through the church window.

Hillier and Hilton

lend a livelier aspect to the whole and are proof that living material is being used.

Ideally, such arrangements should be made just before the event, not only to ensure that the flowers are fresh but also because newly cut foliage gives off a distinctive smell, and this green, lush scent, mixed with the heavy perfume of the blooms, can freshen and enliven the whole church.

The arrangements shown are fixed in a base of foam encased in wire mesh, with two metal tubes pushed into the foam at the back of each container to give additional height and support to the heavy oak branches. The background greenery is positioned first, and then the shape is filled out with flowers. The delicate, grass-like *scirpus variagata* is the finishing touch.

Wedding Flowers

The church event which probably makes the heaviest demands on the flower arranger is a wedding, which is why a variety of wedding flowers is shown on the following pages.

Because of their generally elaborate nature and the many considerations of style, diplomacy and coordination involved, wedding flowers are normally arranged by professional florists. Such an undertaking would be formidable indeed for a rank beginner, but an amateur flower arranger with some experience should be able not only to 'do' the flowers but to express with special clarity the personal style of the bride.

Techniques. Most of the techniques described in this section may of course be used on other occasions: presentation posies and bouquets can be constructed in a similar fashion to brides' bouquets; and pew garlands, possibly in different colours, could decorate a ballroom. The altar flowers could easily be adapted, with the introduction of different material, into arrangements suitable for Easter or Christmas.

Planning. Wedding flowers fall into two groups: the fixed arrangements which decorate the church itself; and the bouquets, posies and garlands for the bride and bridesmaids. When planning wedding flowers it is important to consider the church, the dresses and the bride herself—not only her preferences but her style. As she is to be the centre of the occasion it is essential to decide whether she will best be complemented by flowers which are formal or informal, elegant or pretty, long-stemmed or dainty. It is as much a mistake to dwarf a small bride with huge arrangements and a large bouquet as it is to make a tall bride look disproportionately large against delicate arrangements and a small posy.

Ideally, the church flowers and the bride's flowers should be planned as one continuous scheme so that all the flowers form a cohesive design.

Traditionally, wedding flowers are white, and white flowers effectively lighten a dark church. Yet they do not have to be white, and if the church is a modern one with pale walls and woodwork, a warm pink or peach may look better. Moreover, if the bride is wearing a dress of stark white fabric, white flowers which have a softer and creamier tone may clash with it.

As part of the planning process it is always wise to look round the church to see the type of containers available. One church may have heavy stone containers, capable of supporting a large amount of plant material, while another may have lightweight metal containers on long spindly legs which will tip over if they contain too much tall, thick-stemmed foliage.

Every year, at the feast of Corpus Christi, this solid carpet of flowers is laid down in the central aisle of Arundel cathedral in Sussex. The carpet is 30m (90ft) long and 2m (6ft) wide and is made up of many thousands of blooms laid on a foundation of foliage.

The tradition was introduced by Henry, 15th Duke of Norfolk, in 1873, and the 20 or more parishioners who design and create the carpet have always followed the same simple methods that have been used throughout the years, without the introduction of any modern mechanics.

As Corpus Christi is a movable feast, the choice of flowers varies from year to year and it is always designed with the available blooms borne in mind.

Overleaf: pew decorations adorn a church for a formal wedding. They must be carefully designed so as not to impede the progress of the bridal party, nor to block the entrance of the congregation to the pews.

Pew Decorations

Pew decorations with garland tails give an air of lavish abundance to a ceremony, and carry the scent of flowers right down the aisle. Those in the photograph are placed on each pew end, but the effect is very nearly as good if they are placed on alternate ones.

It will almost certainly be necessary to make these decorations elsewhere and attach them to the pews on the day, in which case it is useful to have a few spare flowers to fill in unexpected gaps or to camouflage the mechanics.

The mechanics consist of a block of prepared foam wired to a plastic saucer, so that the wire criss-crosses the foam to hold it firmly without pulling so tightly that it cuts the foam. Two ends of wire at least 20cm (8in) long are left free at the top of the structure for fixing it to the pew.

The mound of flowers and foliage is arranged in the foam in an oval shape running almost to a point at the bottom, to prepare the eye for the garland to follow. At the planning stage, it is important to consider the size of the flower-oval in relation to the size of the top of the pew, so that it

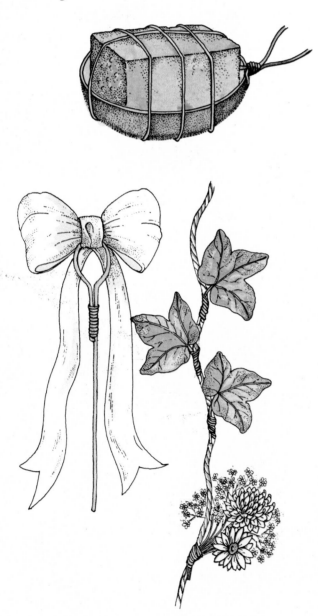

A block of foam wired to a plastic dish is the base of the pew decoration. Bows are tied to looped wire which can be pushed into the foam. Ivy is bound to string, and floral sprigs are attached for the garland tail.

does not look top-heavy. The flowers should not stick out too far or they will make the aisle too narrow for the procession.

The ribbon bows are tied to a loop made at the top of a piece of 0.46mm (26 gauge) wire, which is then pushed deeply into the foam so that the bows and streamers look as if they are made from one continuous length of ribbon.

The garland tail is built on a piece of mossing string cut to the required length, plus enough to tie to the wire on the saucer. A length of ivy is wound around the length of the string, caught with wire where necessary, and the rest of the garland is built sprig by sprig.

The first sprig is made up of a daisy-spray chrysanthemum, with about one centimetre or half an inch of stem, and a piece of gypsophila, bound together with reel wire in such a way that two tails of wire, each about two centimetres (one inch) long, protrude from the sprig. These two tails of wire are used to bind the sprig to the string, with the flowers facing downwards at a slight angle. The next sprig, of gypsophila and one dwarf gladiolus, is smaller and bound in place about five centimetres (two inches) below the first. A garland built in this way can be as long or as bushy as necessary, although, for a trailing garland, it is best to make the sprigs tinier and tinier towards the tip.

Finally, the string-based garland is tied to the saucer-based bunch, and the whole is fixed to the pew end with wire. It is necessary to be extremely careful at this stage because the wire must be bound sufficiently firmly to support the weight of the arrangement. It must not scratch the wood of the pew and must also, if necessary, be hidden by one or two extra blooms or ivy leaves stuck into the back of the arrangement.

Table flowers
The group of traditional white lilies and roses shown below is carefully built into circular form on a plastic foam base. The pointed lilies echo pointed arches above them, while the gently rounded shape of the whole arrangement softens the slightly austere effect of the Gothic window. The theme of white flowers against green oak leaves complements the altar arrangements, and the fact that several different types of flower have been used widens the choice of suitable flowers for a bridal bouquet.

A massed arrangement on a table at the back of the church shows that the decoration has been considered as a whole and all attention has not gone to the altar.

Our Wedding

Bridal Bouquets

A bride's choice of bouquet is such an individual thing that three very different types are described below.

Lily sheaf

This is made of longiflorum lilies, chosen for their good shape. There are nine lilies, including buds, in the sheaf and, ideally, none of them should be wired, although some may have to be so that they can be guided to form the right overall pattern. The flowers are arranged in the hand until a pleasing formation is reached, and their stems are then trimmed. It is important to arrange the blooms so that they are well-spaced, and to make sure that, even when trimmed, the length of the stems is in proportion to the size of the blooms.

The decision about wiring the flowers can only be made when the flowers have been bought and examined to see how they lie together. They are easy to wire, if necessary. A piece of 1.25mm (18 gauge) wire should be pushed up inside each stem to the base of the flower, and reel wire bound firmly around from the base of the flower down to the thinner part of the stem. Gutta-percha should be bound tightly round the wire, with the real stems sticking out at the bottom.

The finished sheaf is bound tightly with gutta-percha and then with ribbon. The bow, with its trailing ends, is tied on later.

This kind of sheaf should only be carried by a tall bride.

Orchid bouquet

This is the most difficult of the bouquets and takes a long time to make because each bloom and leaf is wired separately and each spray then carefully built up from these single wired blooms. The bouquet is made with cybidium orchids, ivy leaves and chincherinchee blossoms.

Wiring. First, each piece of plant material is fixed on long, 0.90mm (20 gauge) wires which may be cut later, as necessary.

The cymbidium orchids are wired in exactly the same way as the lilies in the sheaf already described, and bound with gutta-percha. The ivy leaves are fixed on a hairpin shape which enters the lower centre of each leaf from the back and doubles out again, and the two stems of wire are then bound with reel wire, then gutta percha. Each chincherinchee blossom has a piece of wire pushed through its centre from the back, and the base of the flower is secured to this by reel wire. Each wire is then covered with gutta-percha. The chincherinchee sprays are made up by bringing the gutta-percha-covered 'stems' together in the right formation and twisting them together. (Before attempting to make one of these sprays it is essential to have the overall shape clearly in mind.)

Assembly. Once the sprays, orchids and leaves are fully wired they will bend in any direction. It is important, when you arrange the bouquet in the hand, to lay in the longest blooms first.

The final stems which are to be held by the bride should be gutta-percha'd into a single 'stem'.

Daisy bunch

This is the easiest of the three bouquets to make. It simply consists of daisy-spray chrysanthemums, white pinks, white roses, bridal gladioli, gypsophila and eucalyptus leaves bound together in a slightly dome-shaped bunch. First, one of each kind of flower is bound together with reel wire, and then the remainder of the flowers and foliage is added a piece at a time, at an angle, and bound into place. As each flower is bound in, the bunch is turned slightly, the next flower bound in at an angle, the bunch turned again, and so on. The finished bunch is tied with a simple bow.

This is the simplest of bouquet styles. It is made by binding in the central flowers in a bunch, then adding the others one at a time.

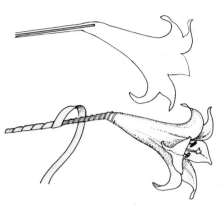

Stub wire is inserted, then stem is taped, but wire is optional.

Ivy is wired, as shown here, with reel wire. Chincherinchee blossoms are wired separately and then bound together.

Hillier and Hilton

Headdress

For a circlet for a small brides-maid it is essential to use very tiny, delicate flowers. These must echo the flowers she carries and so, to a certain extent, the flowers on the head will dictate the flowers to be held in the hand. The choice for this circlet is love-in-a-mist, gypsophila and chin-cherinchee, with a single daisy-spray chrysanthemum as the 'jewel' in the centre of the crown. (Single stock or larkspur flowers and a 'bachelor's button' chry-santhemum would be equally suitable.)

The first step is to make a wire circlet to fit the child's head comfortably. In this case, 0.90mm (20 gauge) stub wires are used. Because one length is not sufficient, two are joined by overlapping the ends and twist-ing them together. The wire is

Twist two stub wires together.

then formed into a circle to fit the head with about three centi-metres (one inch) over at each end. These two extra lengths are used to form a simple hook at

Connect wire ends as shown.

one end and a loop bound in place with a short piece of reel wire at the other. The entire length of wire, including the hook and loop, is then covered with gutta-percha. Winding the

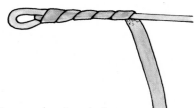

Tape stub wire circlet.

gutta-percha round and round the wire, so that it overlaps itself at an angle, is a fiddly job, but essential. Not only does it hide the wire, making it look like a stalk, but it also protects the head from being scratched.

The circlet is built on the wire base in the same way as the gar-land tail on the pew decorations previously described. Tiny sprigs are formed, bound together with reel wire, and the reel wire is covered with gutta-percha. Each

Bind sprigs with reel wire.

sprig is then bound to the head-band, working from the ends towards the centre.

The chincherinchee flowers are introduced towards the sides and front and are fixed by means of a short piece of wire pushed up the stem into the flower. Love-in-a-mist and gypsophila are bound to the wired stem to form

Cover sprigs with gutta-percha.

a sprig in the usual way.

The central bloom is fixed with a short length of wire pushed up the stem and out through the centre of the flower; the tip of the wire is bent into a tiny hook and the wire pulled gently back down the stem until the hook is firmly and invisibly

Wire central bloom as shown.

lodged among the flowerets. Because this piece of wire does not show, there is no need to cover it with gutta-percha. It can take a lot of patience to bind a central flower in place so that it is exactly central and looking out-wards, not up or down. When the flower is successfully in place, it is quite easy to bend the flowered wire into a circlet and slip the hook into the loop.

Flower Ball

A ball of flowers pleases and interests a small bridesmaid and is less likely to be crushed or dropped than a posy—but it must be strongly made because she will undoubtedly play with it.

The base is a plastic foam ball, in this case about 10 centimetres (four inches) in diameter, decorated with about sixty flower heads. The proportions depend upon the size of the bridesmaid and a smaller arrangement should be made for a very tiny child.

Attach the ribbon with a 0.50mm (24 gauge) stub wire about three times the length of the diameter of the ball. The wire is bent into a hairpin shape with a flat top exactly the width of the ribbon. The wire is then pushed into the ball, with the centre of the length of ribbon trapped beneath the flat top, until the two ends of wire protrude on the other side. These two ends are bent back and pushed into the ball.

The flowers—in this case daisy-spray chrysanthemums and love-in-a-mist—are prepared as follows: the chrysanthemums are cut with about two centimetres (¾ inch) of stem and wired in exactly the same way as the central flower on the circlet opposite, with wire pushed up through the centre, hooked and pulled gently back. The love-in-a-mist is cut to the same length, laid beside a 0.46mm (26 gauge) stub wire, and attached to it by means of a length of reel wire wound round both stem and heavy wire. There is no need to hide the wire with gutta-percha.

The wire 'stems' of the prepared flowers are then pushed firmly into the foam ball until it is covered. Here it is important to know that the wire can only go into the ball up to the end of the flower stem, so the length of the stem has a bearing on the overall size of the finished ball.

When half the ball is covered it becomes impossible to hold, and a kitchen fork with sharp tines can be pushed gently in among the flowers and into the foam so that the ball can be held like a toffee apple and the other side completed.

Finally, the length of ribbon should be adjusted against the bridesmaid herself and a bow tied so that the ball hangs at the right length.

Right: plastic foam ball, wired flower heads, stub wire and ribbon.

A foam ball makes an excellent surface for a pomander, since flowers can be inserted easily.

143

Competitions

There are several reasons for taking up amateur show work, and the possibility of winning a prize is not necessarily the main one. Experience and new ideas are more valuable gains than awards, and most people enjoy the company of others with like interests. If possible, the novice should visit a show before entering one as a competitor, and look carefully at the arrangements and perhaps talk to the exhibitors.

Schedule. Competitions have their own specific rules and conventions and before it is possible to enter a show it is necessary to acquire a copy of the schedule, which will be available from the show secretary. This schedule will contain all the necessary practical information, such as the date, time and place of the show; the various classes; definitions of eligibility to enter; fees payable; and so on. There will also be an entry form which must be completed and returned, together with the fee, by a specific date.

As well as publishing leaflets on show work for beginners, many organizations publish a booklet on the correct interpretation of schedule titles.

Essential equipment. As well as the flowers and their containers, it is usual for competitors to include a backdrop or drape which can be made of card covered with fabric. A flat base or mat on which to set the arrangement is also usual. Sometimes additional accessories such as figurines are allowed (see overleaf).

Fresh fruit can be a far more effective decoration as part of a flower arrangement than in a bowl. The grapes are tied in place and the apples mounted on wire.

Overleaf: two very different interpretations of a competition theme entitled My Fair Lady. One arrangement uses only five blooms while the other is more profuse. In both cases the props are figurines and are an integral part of the design. The background hangings, or drapes as they are sometimes called, have been carefully chosen to show up the flower material to its best advantage. Both these points would be taken into consideration by the judges, as would the choice and arrangement of the plants, and the container.

Measurements. Exhibitors are normally given maximum measurements for the height, width and depth allowed and to disregard these measurements means disqualification.

Classes. It is often possible to enter several classes in a show, but beginners are advised to choose just two: more than this can be too demanding and the newcomer who enters for only one class is in danger of ruining an arrangement by paying too much attention to it.

Each class is given a title—Autumn Abundance, perhaps, or Tranquil Lakeside—or, as illustrated overleaf, My Fair Lady. It is the task of the competitors to interpret the title in plant material, not only imaginatively, but also accurately. An exhibit which does not conform to the stated title will be instantly disqualified.

Planning. It is wise to plan competition exhibits as far in advance as possible; it may be necessary to borrow containers or accessories, and it is certainly necessary to allow time to order or collect plant material. A dress rehearsal is a good idea.

It is also sensible to plan the transportation of material in advance; flowers must be laid end to end in a box; foliage contained within large polythene bags tied at the neck; drapes ironed and rolled on cardboard tubes; and accessories, containers, and mechanics packed into a box or basket. It is also a good idea to mark all equipment to avoid loss, since competitors work very closely together and it is very easy to get belongings mixed up.

Arranging. The actual show piece must be arranged *in situ*, very often with another competitor on either side, which means that not only is there no privacy, but also all flowers and equipment must be contained within quite a small space, even while they are in use. This can be a distracting situation, especially for a beginner, and it is helpful, therefore, to have had a try-out so as to be reasonably confident about the design and the possibility of carrying it through.

The judges' decision is normally based on the following points: that the theme is well-conveyed; the arrangement is well-balanced; the plant material is in good condition; the space allowed is used to good advantage; and any accessory such as a figurine is in scale with the arrangement.

Seasonal Displays

Seasonal displays provide challenging themes for flower arrangers, and festive occasions can often be the time for highly unusual treatments of flowers to convey the spirit of the event.

The two arrangements featured here are obviously Christmas displays, although the holly-filled candelabra could be used throughout the winter. The nativity scene is built of a polystyrene base on to which a 2.5 centimetre (one inch) cube of floral foam has been mounted. The raffia is attached to stub wires. The other components are holly, chrysanthemums, glycerined leaves, ribbon, the Christmas figures and a star made of cardboard and glitter.

Seasonal festivities provide arrangers with challenging opportunities for using flowers as expressions of the occasion, and the symbolism which certain flowers have traditionally—such as holly for Christmas—can be used to this end. A variety of displays can result, even using the same material. Two Christmas displays shown here, for example, have very different styles, yet both use the same sort of materials and both are built on floral foam.

Daphne Ramsbottom

Ikebana

Ikebana is known in the west as the art of Japanese flower arrangement, but the word actually means 'the arrangement of living plant material'—a more suitable title because traditional Japanese arrangements do not use many flowers but are created principally with branches and grasses. In contrast to western styles, the emphasis is on line rather than on colour, and on simplicity rather than on abundance.

The art of Ikebana was born in Buddhist temples, where it was customary to place an offering of flowers before the statue of the Buddha. Legend suggests that the very first flower arrangements were created from storm-scattered branches

The Rikka arrangement, standing in a copper container on a vermillion lacquered base, was created with cherry, camellia and forsythia by Soshoen Yokachi, Head Master of the Soami School, Tokyo. These huge temple styles were later modified into Shoka (above) to suit a domestic environment.

and flowers which the monks rescued and put in water to give them a few hours more life. Later, plant material was deliberately cut, but great care was always taken to ensure that the cut material would live for as long as possible.

In the sixth century a priest called Ono-no-Imoko developed the fundamentals of Ikebana, as essentially an arrangement which symbolizes the living universe in its spiritual and physical manifestations. In order that the arrangement should be harmonious, it was believed to be necessary to approach it with a peaceful mind, so that the work itself constituted a form of prayer or meditation. For centuries the art belonged only to the priests, and although modern Ikebana is very different from the temple arrangements, it has carried with it, through all its evolutions of style, the original spiritual significance and its ability to bring peace and tranquility both to those who create the arrangements and to those who enjoy them.

The true study of Ikebana is a way of life. It is said that it takes at least five years to train a teacher but that not even a Grand Master would consider his training to be complete. This sounds very solemn and daunting, especially to the western mind. But Ikebana exists on various levels—it is not only a serious spiritual exercise, it is also a happy art, fun to do and pleasant to look at. A novice, working on his or her first arrangement, will derive great enjoyment from both the effort and the result; if the piece falls rather far short of the work of a master, fire will not strike from heaven.

Types of Arrangement

Rikka or Rikkwa—literally 'standing up plant cuttings'—was the name given to the earliest temple arrangements. They stood in great bronze urns and were always large, but as time went on they were sometimes created as much as six metres (20 feet) high and took many days to arrange. Entirely suited to their own situation, these arrangements would be impractical for use in the

A Shoka arrangement of Iris laevigata in a Mashikoware container on a lacquered base, created by Soshoen Yokachi. Both Rikka and Shoka are early classical styles.

home and are beyond the scope of anyone but a Master (see previous page).

Shoka or Seika is the name of the style which evolved to meet domestic needs when the art moved from temple to home. Although simpler than Rikka, Shoka arrangements were still large, still based in heavy vases, and appeared only in the homes of noblemen and warriors. At this stage in its development the art was practised exclusively by men.

Nageire—literally 'thrown in'—is the style which evolved when Ikebana was taken up in ordinary homes and, as Nageire grew in popularity, women were gradually admitted to the art. A Nageire arrangement requires an upright container, and is an extremely simplified form of Shoka.

Moribana—or 'flowers piled up'—was developed in the 1860s when western culture, including styles of flower arrangement, began to affect Japanese culture. It is the most popular style outside Japan, and is also the style for the beginner who, traditionally, is guided backwards through the development of Ikebana and only introduced to Rikka at a very advanced stage. A Moribana arrangement requires a flat container.

Sogetsu School

There are literally hundreds of schools of Ikebana. The largest of the modern schools is the Sogetsu, founded in the 1920s by Sofu Toshigahara, to break away from the difficult classical styles. Although it teaches the traditional basic principles, and its tenets are acceptable even to the Grand Masters of other schools, its more modern and relaxed approach makes it the most suited to western beginners. The general guide for the beginner contained in this chapter is based on the work of this school.

Both Moribana and Nageire, as taught by the Sogetsu school throughout the west, are suited to modern western homes in which simplicity and clear lines are increasingly popular. The creation of such arrangements is also immensely effective in unravelling the tensions and anxieties of modern life. It is not possible to build up a harmonious arrangement in a hurry, and the necessity of settling down quietly with the material, to understand its

In this modern free-style arrangement the foliage is supported in a well-kenzan which is hidden in a hollow of the driftwood container. Like the designs on the following pages, it was created by Stella Coe.

natural lines and to see how best to use them, is just the kind of soothing, relaxing occupation which is so sorely needed today.

Symbolism

Symbolism is an important aspect of Ikebana but the western mind usually tries to understand symbolism in a logical and intellectual manner, when it can be truly understood only from the heart. Although particular flowers and stems do have particular meanings, it is not helpful to offer a list because the meanings are not rigid and it is the feeling of the whole arrangement which is important rather than the meaning of an individual part of it. What is more, some of the symbolism may be personal to the arranger—for instance, an arrangement made with a particular person in mind would probably include his or her favourite flower. In general, grasses and branches are masculine and flowers feminine; lines which droop are sad and lines which lift are happy; bare branches speak of desolation and winter; black stems bearing blossom speak of spring, reawakening and hope; and richly leafed stems speak of summer and abundance.

Equipment

Tool kits. It is possible to buy a five-piece Japanese tool kit for Ikebana. This consists of a small chopper for cutting large branches, a saw for slightly thinner branches, a double-edged knife for trimming, a pair of springless shears (which are less tiring to use than those with springs) and a small syringe which can be used to inject water into hollow stems and also to spray the finished arrangement. This tool kit is a pleasant thing to own but is not essential, and it is probably a mistake to spend a great deal of money on equipment in the early stages.

Scissors. The one essential is a pair of strong, sharp scissors—preferably Japanese scissors or springless shears which make it possible to cut without tensing the muscles.

Kenzans, or pinholders, have already been discussed on page 46 but there are various sizes and shapes available specially for Ikebana. Each one is suitable for a particular type of plant material and arrangement.

A useful all-purpose kenzan is circular with close-set pins of medium length; longer pins are useful for fleshy stems; a kenzan with a central *shippo*, or stem-supporter, is helpful to hold large branches. A well-kenzan has its own built-in water-container and can be used in basket arrangements; a combined sun and moon kenzan is necessary for divided arrangements; and tiny kenzans support individual flowers.

It is a good idea to build up a collection so that the ideal kenzan is always available; but it is important to buy top-quality kenzans with heavy lead bases. A cheap one is a false economy. Unlike the pinholders used in western flower arrangements, these will often have to support the weight of a heavy branch arranged with its centre of gravity well beyond the kenzan itself. If the kenzan is too light the arrangement will simply collapse. (If a branch is too heavy even for a lead-based kenzan, it is quite permissible to weight it with a second kenzan placed upside down upon it so that the pins interlock. But it is not permissible to use any means to stick the kenzan to the bottom of the container. This is because it must always be pos-

Equipment for Ikebana: left, a selection of shippos and kenzans, including a circular and semi-circular sun and moon kenzan; right, some tools—a knife, springless shears, a handsaw, syringe and chopper.

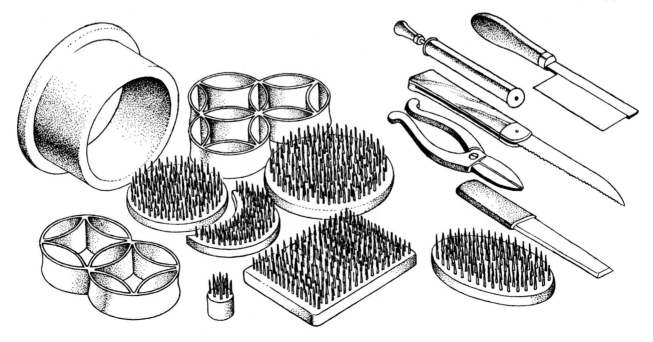

sible to shift the entire arrangement within the container, even if only by an infinitesimal amount, to improve the balance of the finished work.)

Containers. Basically, Nageire containers are tall and narrow and Moribana containers are shallow and dish-like but capable of containing water at least seven centimetres (three inches) deep. The container should always blend with the arrangement and there are two useful points to bear in mind to ensure that this happens: one is that, traditionally, containers are seasonal, just as plant material is seasonal; metal containers suit winter arrangements, pottery or lacquer containers suit spring and autumn arrangements, and basket containers suit summer arrangements. The other point is that the colours of containers should be unobtrusive— the colours of earth, bark, sand and dark foliage.

Bases. Baskets should stand on their own, but it is customary to place most other containers on a base; a round or irregular base for a square container and a square or rectangular base for a round container. This base might be a piece of natural wood, a bamboo mat, a Japanese lacquer base, a shaped clay base or even a slab of marble. The proportions of base to container should be pleasing and the container should be placed asymmetrically on the chosen base.

A collection of containers, both classical and modern. On the right, the bamboo raft makes an attractive base, and the gold fan can be used as a backing behind an arrangement. Some of the earliest arrangements stood in dark temples and castles and the use of gold developed to brighten the corner where the foliage stood.

Plant Material

Very little material is necessary, which means that Ikebana is an exceptionally economical form of decoration. It also means that for a special occasion it is possible to buy just one or two rare and beautiful blooms. Traditionally, the arrangement should reflect its surroundings and the spirit of its creator, and in many ways the most suitable material comes from the garden of the house where the arrangement is to stand—especially if part of the garden is visible from the room housing the arrangement. However, the rooms in many western homes are somewhat cut off from the outside world, in that they do not have a view of trees and flowers, and a great many people live in flats and apartments with no gardens. Because of this it is permissible to choose other than strictly local material, and even to use exotic flowers. Choice will be determined by the effect required. For 'every day', material in season is best, and it is undoubtedly more satisfying to go into the countryside at a weekend and choose one or two branches that appeal than simply to visit the local florist. On the other hand, many modern florists have a wide range of material, both seasonal and forced, available at any time and they are usually prepared to sell small amounts, a few willow stems, a single rose, and so on.

Caring for plant material

Ideally, flowers and branches should be cut in the early morning or the early evening, when the sap is flowing. If at all possible, stand each stem in water within seconds of severing it from the parent plant. If the plant material has had to travel, whether from the country, the garden or the florist, the stems should be put into a bowl of water and the last three centimetres (one inch) or so cut off, diagonally, below water level. Stems which have been cut straight across will stand flat on the bottom of the container and be less able to draw up water.

To help preserve flowers and leaves, stems which bleed a milky substance when cut should be briefly singed in a flame; other stems should be dipped into boiling water (see chapter four for details). In each case, wrap the bloom gently in tissue paper.

It is vital that the arrangement stands in pure, clean water. Containers and kenzans must be absolutely spotless.

Trimming. Not so much as a single leaf should lie below water level, where it will rot and pollute the water. It is therefore essential to trim away from branches and stems any leaves or buds which would otherwise be below the waterline, simply in order to keep the water pure. It is also necessary to trim away any twigs or leaves which interfere with the line of the arrangement. It is best to do this trimming when the material is fixed in position because only then is it possible to see what should be removed. The natural line of most growing plant material leads it upwards, towards the sun, and the same should be true of cut material in a container. If a branch is required to droop downwards, it is always possible to trim it back to the last uplifted leaf so that the downward curve has a slight upward trend at the end.

Fixing Material

In *Moribana*, which is arranged in a flat container, the material must be fixed into a kenzan. Branches should be pressed down on to the pins, with the cut edge of the stem uppermost, and then angled as required. Flower stems should be placed at the correct angle and pressed until pierced by the pins. In the case of a very thin or flimsy stem, cut a short length of a fleshy stem and insert the thin stem into it, thus giving the thin stem a firm base.

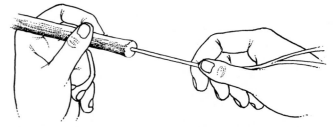

Pushing a flimsy stem into a piece of strong stem.

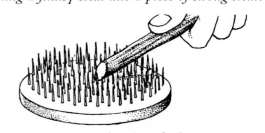

Pressing a stem on to the pins of a kenzan.

In *Nageire*, which is arranged in a tall, narrow container, the kenzan is obviously of no use, and there are three different methods of keeping the material in place.

One of the simplest is the 'vertical fixture'. This involves cutting a piece of branch until it is about two thirds of the height of the container and then making a split down its centre for about seven centimetres (three inches), so that it is forked. This branch should stand diagonally across the inside of the container, forked end uppermost. The bottom of the first branch to be positioned should be split in exactly the same way and the forked ends of the two branches interlocked. This makes a very secure base for the placing of other material.

The 'crossbar' fixture is suitable for cylindrical containers and consists of two twigs cut to size so

Three ways of fixing plant material for a Nageire arrangement. Left to right: vertical fixture, cross-bar fixture and single bar fixture.

that they fit snugly about three centimetres (one inch) below the rim of the container in the form of a cross. Branches can then be placed so that their stem ends rest against the inside of the container and the body of their weight rests against the cross-bar.

The 'single bar' fixture is a twig inserted horizontally into a split made in the end of a branch so that when the branch is placed in the container, the twig supports it by resting against the walls of the container.

Bending. It is quite permissible to improve the shape of a branch or stem by bending it if a curve is natural to it (a willow stem or an iris leaf may be bent, but an iris or a gladiolus bloom must remain straight). With a little practice, it is possible to bend a branch without breaking it, if it has sap in it. The stem should be held in such a way that the thumbs

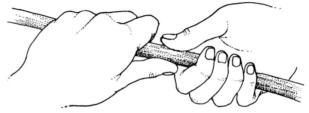

To bend a stem, hold it so that the thumbs are one above the other, with the stem between, and bend it with a slight twisting movement.

lie one above the other with the stem between them. It can then be bent and massaged very gently with a slight twisting movement which will break some of the fibres inside it. This is important because if the internal fibres are not broken the stem will simply straighten out again in water.

Location

It is important to decide where the arrangement is to stand before beginning work on it, because it must be created *in situ*. When deciding, consider the effect on the plant material itself and do not place it in a draught, over a radiator or fire, or in direct sunlight.

In Japan, the arrangement is placed in the Tokonoma, or recess, which is about two metres (six feet) wide and one metre (three feet) deep, and which is often backed by a hanging picture. In a western home the arrangement should, ideally, be placed against a plain wall but, if this is not possible, a plain piece of fabric hanging behind the arrangement will also enable its form to be seen clearly.

Because it is so deeply concerned with the forms, angles and spatial relationships of plant material, the study and practice of Ikebana enriches the awareness of the natural world. Each landscape and every tree and plant can be seen as Ikebana which, once it has raised the perception, will never allow it to atrophy again.

Basic Forms

There are two basic forms of arrangement, the upright (Risshin Kei) and the slanting (Keishin Kei). Both Moribana and Nageire can take an upright or a slanting form, depending on the type of material available and the effect sought. It is the position of the longest branch (Shin) which determines the form the arrangement will take. In an upright arrangement it should be at an angle of 10° to an imaginary vertical line drawn from its base; in a slanting arrangement the angle should be 45°. A protractor may be used to measure angles correctly.

Positioning material

An Ikebana arrangement, whether it is Nageire or Moribana, symbolizes the living universe by representing what are seen as its three principal aspects: Heaven (Shin), Man (Soe) and Earth (Hikae), represented diagrammatically as Shin=○; Soe=□; Hikae=△. The branches or flowers which symbolize these three are always positioned

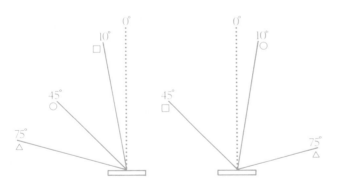

Both upright and slanting styles use the same three basic angles for the placement of the plant material.

first, and any additional materials (Jushi) are placed later. There are rules which govern the length of each of the main branches, both in relation to each other and in relation to the size of the container, and also rules which govern the angles of the branches in relation to the imaginary vertical line rising from the base of Shin; but these rules are, within reason, flexible. They should be regarded as helpful guidelines rather than rigid laws.

Length. In a standard arrangement, the length of Shin, the principal line, should be the width of the

container plus the depth and half as much again. Soe should measure three quarters of Shin and Hikae should measure three quarters of Soe. Jushi, which can be used to supplement any of the main lines or to hide the kenzan, should never be as long as the stems they supplement and must be cut to varying lengths to avoid the static look of symmetry.

Angles. The angles differ in upright and horizontal styles—in the upright style the tip of the longest branch, Shin, should be at an angle of 10°. The other two angles, of 45° and 75°, are interchangeable between Soe and Hikae—in other words, if Soe is at 75°, Hikae must be at 45°, and vice versa. In the slanting style, Shin is at an angle of 45°, and Soe and Hikae are interchangeable at 10° and 75°.

Tranquillity. *An upright Moribana arrangement: the iris leaves are placed first, their satisfying curves encouraged by gentle stroking between the first and second fingers. The flowers and buds are placed next, and the hosta leaves, whose functions are to lend weight to the base of the arrangement and to camouflage the kenzans and the leggy lily stems, are placed last.*

Celebration. *This is a Nageire slanting style arrangement in a pair of Japanese pottery containers on a random-shaped wooden base. Two miniature lacquered screens add weight to the base and prevent it from looking top-heavy. It was designed by Stella Coe to celebrate the Sogetsu school's 50th anniversary, and this explains the use of the gold-sprayed branch, since gold is traditionally used in celebration arrangements.*

It is what is known as an 'arrangement of humility' because the Soe line, representing man, is omitted. The main branch leaning to the right is Shin at 45° and the two carnations which are almost upright on the left are Hikae at 10°. The rest of the leaves and flowers are Jushi, supporting the main lines. The small branch which has been allowed to droop across the right hand container, to link it with the left, has been trimmed so that despite its downward slant it has an upward movement.

It has been suggested that the appearance of gold in traditional arrangements originated in the dark temples and castles of Japan where, before the days of electric light, the gold was used to reflect back the few rays of sun which penetrated the gloom, and so make the branches more clearly visible. Even today some arrangers stand a huge gold paper fan behind a finished piece of work to throw it into sharp relief.

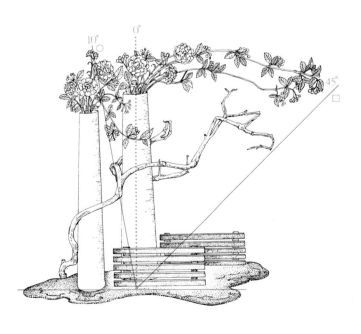

Dynamic Peace. *This is a simple upright Moribana arrangement in a circular lacquer container which is standing on two bamboo rafts. That it is a summer arrangement is shown by the lushness of the foliage, the presence of the roses, and the area of cool water visible in the container, whose colour suggests a deep pool. In summer it is correct to show a wide area of water; in autumn or winter the least possible area should be visible because the sight of water in winter has a chilling effect on the spirit.*

In this arrangement, the tall curving branch is Shin, at 10°, the smaller branch to the right is Soe at 45°, and the rose to the far left is Hikae at 75°. The other four roses are Jushi, three of them placed in a line to supplement Shin, and one at the base of Hikae to lend a little necessary weight. As the days pass, the roses will open more fully and the arrangement will change slightly in appearance and character, but this will not matter. The most important aspect of any arrangement is that it is a living thing, and any natural changes which occur are entirely acceptable.

Winter's Moon. *The overall colouring and the drooping leaves of the chrysanthemum create a feeling of desolation, but the spiky branches—indicative of hard frost and sharp cold—are vigorous, even a little dangerous, and their clenched buds promise that, whatever the opposition, there will be a spring awakening.*

The Japanese moon container is carved from wood, and, since the moon hangs alone, it has no base.

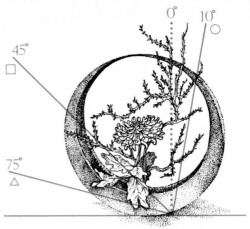

The Living Image of Space *is a modern free-style arrangement, combining Moribana and Nageire. The branch which links the two parts of the design is Soe at 45°. This branch, in the tall container, was placed first, supported by a forked twig, and the branch in its turn formed the support for the flowers. A kenzan holds the stems in the small container. The two bread baskets are an integral part of the design and their patterns give a sense of movement to the whole.*

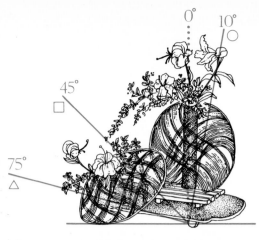

Preserved Flowers

Preserving plants is an ancient practice that has again come into fashion, and with good reason, since the benefits to be accrued from this simple craft are many, and of particular interest to flower arrangers.

Advantages of Preserved Arrangements

Dried flowers can be arranged in much the same way as fresh flowers, but there are some obvious differences and advantages in using dried material.

First of all, dried flower arrangements do not need looking after: vases do not have to be topped up with water or scrubbed clean after use; and there are no wilted blooms to remove.

Secondly, there are wider decorative uses for dried plants and flowers for, as well as making conventional 'cut flower' arrangements, they can be assembled into three-dimensional collages or used to make pressed flower pictures or even serve as souvenirs such as a bridal bouquet or bridegroom's buttonhole, which can be preserved as mementos to show one's grandchildren.

Dried materials can also be used to make 'fantasy flowers' by wiring together bits of several different plants to make unique 'blooms' for arrangements.

Finally, working with dried plants not only gives one the pleasure of producing something decorative, but there is the additional satisfaction of halting nature's laws of decay and creating out of the ephemeral something long-lasting which will be a source of satisfaction for many years.

Once plants have been preserved they can be stored indefinitely and then used to decorate rooms throughout the autumn and winter, when fresh flowers are no longer available. Clearly, a display of preserved flowers is invaluable during the colder months when the garden is bare and florist's flowers are expensive and often lacking in variety.

Some people prefer to leave dried arrangements in place throughout the year, particularly the more sculptural ones or those which fill a void which a fresh arrangement could not do. But this is a matter of personal choice and dried arrangements can be easily dismantled, stored and re-arranged for the following autumn. Methods of storing preserved material are described further on.

Preserving Methods

The methods of preserving plants are remarkably simple. The raw materials are of course readily available, since flowers and foliage may be collected in the garden or countryside, and gathering them is an enjoyable occupation in itself. The process is not very time-consuming and it can be carried out at leisure throughout the spring and summer months. Virtually anything that grows can be preserved, and some species can be preserved in more ways than one.

The methods of preserving plants fall into two categories: drying and water replacement. The first category, that of drying, includes air drying, pressing and using a drying agent, or desiccant. The second category involves replacing the water in a plant with glycerine. The method chosen will depend on the type of plant and, to some degree, on the time and space available.

Air drying needs a dark, shady place where flowers can be hung for at least a week, and in a small flat or apartment this could be a problem. Flowers which have a natural tendency to dry on their own are best for air drying.

Pressed flowers, on the other hand, need only a press, but the process is long and slow. Pressing is only really possible with flat, thin plant material, with not too high a moisture content.

Drying in a desiccant requires a great deal of space in which to store boxes or tins. In general, desiccants are more suitable for fragile blooms, especially spring flowers, and are very good for retaining a flower's original colours.

The glycerine method requires room for jars and is a comparatively slow method. It is most commonly used for leaves but a few flowers and seed heads also respond to this treatment fairly well.

The methods described here are guidelines, however: no two flowers will be picked at exactly the same time in their life cycles, in exactly the same conditions of climate. There are charts on pages 214–217 which recommend a method for different plants, but experimentation is required for preserving flowers and it is best to try different methods and amass your own set of rules.

To dry flowers on a large scale, you need plenty of room. Choose a method to suit your lifestyle.

Picking

Whichever method of preservation is used, the time to pick plant material is the same. Always pick flowers and foliage at the peak of condition. Pick flowers when the sap is still rising, but before the flowers become fully developed. Cut grasses before they go to seed, and seed heads when they are ripe, just opening, and crisp to the touch. Avoid flowers or foliage which are in any way damaged.

If you intend to use any of the drying methods, it is important to pick on a dry day, after the dew has evaporated, as this accelerates the dehydration process which in turn encourages better colour retention. Once the plants are cut, the process of drying must be begun immediately, before they have time to wilt.

Branches which are to receive glycerine treatment, on the other hand, are best conditioned in deep water for several hours before being preserved. (See chapter three for information on conditioning.)

Air Drying

This is the easiest and most popular method of drying flowers and grasses. It needs no special preparation or equipment, simply enough space and hooks or a line from which to hang stems.

Choosing plant material.

Plants with strong, rigid tissue, such as pampas grass, delphiniums and lavender, are the best ones for air drying because they will keep their shape. Many flowers have a natural tendency to dry on the parent plant outside but they are obviously subject to damage from harsh weather conditions and are therefore better off in a dry, mild atmosphere indoors. Some flowers—the everlastings, for example, such as the type in the picture opposite—are grown especially for their tendency to dry. They are usually hardy or half-hardy annuals and are very easy to grow in a garden. Seed heads and grasses also dry particularly well. Leaves, on the other hand, do not dry well, but shrivel up and lose their shape. Many stems shrivel completely, and the flowers need to be wired (see later), either before or after drying.

Preparation
Pick plants at their peak of condition, and preferably on a dry day. If this is not possible, remove as much moisture as you can with blotting paper. Cut the stems as long as possible, unless the flowers are to be wired before drying. They can always be cut short later, before they are arranged.

How to dry
Pull or cut off all the leaves, which can either be saved for preserving by another method, or discarded.

Drying upside down. Arrange flowers in small bunches—preferably according to variety—and tie them fairly tightly. Bunches of heavier plant material with tougher stems should be tied with

Air drying flowers upside down keeps stems straight.

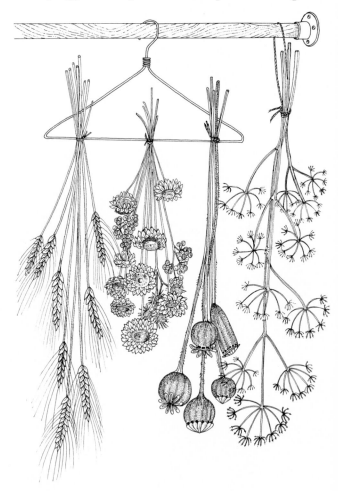

smooth-textured string or gardener's twine which is less likely to damage stems than coarse string. Lighter bunches can be tied with soft silk or nylon thread or fine twine.

Tie with a small loop by which to hang the bunch. If the flowers crowd each other, space them out by pulling the stems to different lengths so that air can circulate round each flower head.

Hang the bunches upside down on hooks, a line, or coat-hangers. Ideally, plant material should be hung in a cool, dry, dark place. These conditions encourage the dehydration process and colour retention. Remember, it is essential that the flower heads have air circulating around them, so hang the bunches well apart.

Bunches may need to be re-tied as they dry because the stems will tend to shrivel and may fall out. Always tighten gently. Hanging upside down helps to keep stems straight and to preserve the shape of the flower heads.

Drying upright. Some plants are best dried upright, especially those with firm, upright stems and rounded flower clusters such as cow-parsley Queen Anne's lace and fennel. Fluffy-headed grasses also dry better upright. The stems tend to settle with a slight curve and this may be preferred for certain arrangements. Simply arrange the stems loosely in a tall, fairly narrow-necked container.

N.B. Some people recommend dipping flower heads in alum or borax before drying them as this helps to prevent fading. Shake off the powder before arranging.

Many flowers keep their colours after air drying and make rich, glowing arrangements. Those flowers which have a natural tendency to dry respond best.

Wiring. The stems of many dried flowers are not usable as they become shrivelled and brittle, and flower heads must therefore be wired before they can be arranged.

It is better to wire flowers before they are dried for two reasons. First, it is more difficult to push a wire into a hard, dried flower centre; and second, the flower—and what remains of the stem—tend to shrink during the drying process and to close on the wire, thereby making it firm and secure.

Stub wires, available from florists, come in different gauges and lengths and are described in detail on page 51, but the most commonly used stub wires for dried flowers are 0.90mm and 0.71mm (20 and 22 gauge), and 25cm (10in) in length.

Cut off most of the stem, make a hook in one end of a stub wire and push the other end down through the centre of the flower head (as described on page 51).

An alternative method to this is to push one end of the stub wire up through what remains of the stem into the base of the flower; do not push too hard, or the wire will project from the flower centre and show.

After wiring, false stems can then be covered either with a dry, hollow stem, such as a corn stalk, or with florist's tape, known as gutta-percha. This is made of rubber, but looks like fabric, and is self-adhesive and easy to apply. It comes in several colours; choose a colour with the flower heads and the desired effect in mind.

Some stems will dry successfully, but should nevertheless be wired, either to reinforce them or to give them a slight curve so that they do not appear too stiff. Again, it is better to wire before drying so that the stem shrinks and clings to the wire. The fluffy-headed grasses, for example, which tend to be top-heavy, should have stub wires inserted into their stems up to about half their length, to prevent them from bending over and snapping.

Many of the everlastings are easy to grow in the garden. Dried flowers do eventually fade if exposed to strong sunlight, so grow a fresh supply each year. Once dried, the stems of many flowers become brittle and rather unattractive, so flower heads often need to be wired.

Timing. This varies according to the plant material itself, how full of moisture it was when it was picked, and the atmosphere in which it is dried. Fragile material and grasses usually only take about a week, whereas large, moist flowers can take up to three weeks.

Test the plant material now and again. It is ready when it feels absolutely dry and papery. No harm can be done if you leave it too long, so it is better to err on this side.

Loss of shape. If flowers lose their shape through being crushed, either during the air drying process or while they are stored afterwards, this can be rectified by steaming. Simply hold the flower head over the spout of a boiling kettle for a few seconds, while gently encouraging the flower to re-adopt its former shape with your fingers.

Drying in Water

Plants with exceptionally strong stems, such as yarrow, hydrangeas and many grasses, prefer to be dried gradually while the stem ends are in water. They should be picked when the flower is already just beginning to dry on the parent plant. Then stand the flower, on its own stem, in two centimetres (half an inch) of water, and do not top it up when the water has been absorbed.

Drying in Hot Air

Flowers which are prone to lose their colour (delphiniums, larkspur and the flowers of the globe artichoke, for example, are best dried quickly in hot dry air. Hang the flowers upside down or spread them out on paper on a shelf in a dark airing cupboard, or put them in a box and set it on a radiator. The drying process should only take a few days, depending on the heat and on the condition of the flowers. Check plants frequently and remove them as soon as they feel dry and papery and the petals sound like tissue paper when gently touched.

A simple, casual arrangement of everlastings. The contrasting colours of the vase, the rich bronze of the flowers and their background and the soft pool of lamplight all contribute to make a decorative display.

Susan Gaskell

Desiccants

A desiccant is a substance which withdraws moisture. The most commonly used desiccants are crystals—borax, alum, sand, and silica gel, as well as the proprietary mixtures on the market such as Lasting Flower. Flowers are buried in the desiccant and left in an airtight container until all their moisture has been withdrawn.

Flowers and plants dried with desiccants can last for many years but they are often fragile and need great care. This is a method for those with patience and a light touch.

Choosing plant material
Chemical drying does not work very well on foliage, but many flowers retain both colour and shape extremely well using this method. In general, dahlias and most spring flowers dry well in desiccants.

Colour retention is usually good using desiccants, as long as flowers are kept out of strong sunlight once they have been dried. Dark colours generally fade less quickly than light ones. Reds and purples are very successful and tend to get darker. Very pale yellow or white flowers have a tendency to go brown in the centre and so are better dried quickly in a warm place, such as on top of a boiler.

Picking
Pick flowers on a dry day, after the dew has evaporated. Choose flowers which are not yet fully blown, and do not waste time on imperfect specimens.

Choosing a desiccant
Which desiccant to use is largely a matter of personal choice and it is worth experimenting with different flowers and different desiccants until you discover what works best for you. It is useful to keep a record for future reference of the type of flower, the desiccant used, and the time taken for the process to work. One important consideration

An elegant display combining desiccated dahlias dried in sand and air-dried bachelor's buttons. The outline materials are pressed Senecio greyi and Cytisus batterdieri.

is that the size of grain used must be right for the type of flower: the petals must be supported by the dry medium but they must not be crushed by its weight.

The time necessary for flowers to dry depends on the desiccant used, as well as on the plant material and the warmth of the room, so this may also influence choice.

Silica gel is the most expensive desiccant but it is popular because it acts quickly—in 48 to 72 hours. This short time helps to retain the flowers' original colours, but plant material can become very brittle if immersed for too long.

Silica gel is heavier than other desiccants and is therefore only suitable for stronger tissues (see the dried flower guide, pages 214–217). Crystals may be bought from pharmacists and can be crushed with a rolling pin to make finer grain. Fine crystals may also be bought under brand names such as Lasting Flower.

Silica gel cannot be re-used if the crystals contain a lot of water. An indicator is sold with silica gel which turns blue when it is ready for use, and pink if it is not. Before re-using the gel, place it in the oven at $130°C$ ($250°F$), Gas Mark $\frac{1}{2}$ to dry it out. Remove the crystals when the indicator burns blue after being put into the centre. Do not touch the crystals for some time after this, as they retain heat.

Borax and alum. Fine, delicate plant material needs the lightest of all desiccants, borax or alum. Both of these are inexpensive powders, available from pharmacists. Borax and alum are too fine, however, to support heavier flower petals such as dahlias and they do not penetrate cavities easily, so special care must be taken to ensure that the powder covers all parts of every petal.

The length of time borax and alum take depends on the flowers used and the warmth of the atmosphere, but in general seven to ten days should be allowed.

Alum and borax can be used separately or mixed in equal proportions. Borax on its own tends to cling to the dried petals. Borax can also be mixed with sand—two parts borax to one part sand—to make it heavier if more support is needed to hold petals in position. Borax and alum can be dried after use in an airing cupboard or other warm, dry place.

Sand. This has been used as a drying agent for flowers for centuries. It flows well and so runs easily into cavities between petals. It gives good support to heavier flowers as it is the heaviest desiccant of all. It should therefore not be used with delicate flowers unless mixed with borax as described above. Sand is also the slowest desiccant. In fact, flowers may be left indefinitely in sand, and all will take at least 14 days. Many people claim that the best sand of all comes from Salt Lake City, Utah.

Flowers dried in sand retain their texture and gloss. Better colours are obtained by mixing a table-spoon of bicarbonate of soda to 7kg (15lb) of sand.

Preparation. One disadvantage of using sand, which may discourage the impatient, is that it must be cleaned before use. Fill a bucket three-quarters full of sand and add water to the top. Stir and allow the sand to settle, then remove any floating debris.

Pour off the water and repeat the process several times with clean water. Dry sand in a warm oven at 130°C (250°F), Gas Mark ½ for several hours and sift before use.

Re-use. Sand must be dried in the oven after each use, but it will not need cleaning again.

Wiring

Stems dried in desiccants become very brittle and flower heads must be wired. It is probably easier to wire flower heads before drying, as they are less fragile in their fresh, supple state, but some experts prefer to do it afterwards.

Wiring is done in exactly the same way as for air-dried flowers. Simply make a small hook in one end of a stub wire and push the other end down through the flower head. Alternatively, push a stub wire up through the stem end. (For more details on wiring, see chapter four.)

If wiring is done before dehydration, coil the wire below the flower so that the flower head can sit on the desiccant.

How to use desiccants

Whichever desiccant is used, the procedure is the same.

Flowers should be dried in an airtight container such as a cake or biscuit tin, a plastic, lidded box or a cardboard box which can be sealed up with adhesive tape. Cover the base of the box with a three centimetre (one inch) layer of desiccant, and shake the box gently to level it off. Then place the flower head on top of the desiccant. If several flowers are to be dried in the same box, they should be placed so that they do not touch, and they should be of the same variety, or at least need a similar length of time in the desiccant.

Pour more desiccant gently over the flowers. Lift each petal gently as you pour, or 'dress' the flower using a skewer or toothpick, to make sure all cavities are filled. This will help the flower keep its shape and ensure even drying.

Continue adding desiccant until each flower is covered by about a three centimetre (one inch)

Place flowers on a bed of desiccant and gently pour more desiccant over the petals.

When ready, carefully pour off the desiccant until the dried flower, or flowers, drop into the hand.

layer. Put on an airtight lid—seal with adhesive tape if necessary—and label the container with the contents and the date, and store in a warm, dry place such as an airing cupboard.

When the flower seems ready (see page 175 for the time needed with each type of desiccant), pour off the desiccant in a steady stream through your fingers until a flower drops into your hand. If the petals feel dry and crisp, like paper, the flower is ready and any loose particles of desiccant should be brushed away with a soft paintbrush.

If the flower is not ready, return the flower head to the box and re-cover with desiccant for a little longer. If any petals have come away, they can be

stuck back with a transparent adhesive such as UHU.

Dull petals may be given a sheen by brushing on a little oil. If the petals have a wrinkled appearance, it is probably because the desiccant was not heavy enough. A heavier medium should be used next time to preserve the same kind of flower.

An all-white bouquet is just one way of demonstrating the decorative potential of dried plants. This one contains Bristol fairy, sea lavender, delphiniums, daisies, Fiori catone and kumasasa leaves. To bleach these leaves, dip them in household bleach for a few minutes and then dry them.

Dean at Lennie's

Glycerine

Glycerine can be used to preserve many varieties of foliage which could otherwise only be preserved by pressing. The advantage of glycerined leaves over pressed ones (described further on) is that the former retain their suppleness and are far more realistic and pliable in arrangements. (Pressed leaves tend to look flat and lifeless and they must be wired, whereas glycerined leaves retain their stems, which adds to their natural appearance.)

Glycerine absorption involves replacing the water in plants with glycerine and the result is virtually everlasting, especially in the case of plants with tougher leaves, such as beech.

Colouring

An interesting aspect of glycerine treatment is that the natural colours are not retained—leaves always change their colour and usually become a soft cream, brown, dark red or even purple. It is possible to experiment by adding dyes to the glycerine to obtain different colours, and glycerined leaves can be made to fade by placing them in strong sunlight for a few days. Beech leaves, for example, will turn a pale tan colour, and aspidistra a pale honey.

Choosing material

While it is best suited for preserving leaves, there are a few species of flower and seed head which respond to glycerine (see Flower Guide). Both deciduous and evergreen foliage, as well as many houseplant leaves, can be glycerined successfully. Very fragile leaves, such as lime, however, are not suitable. Beech leaves are most commonly used for this method. Individual leaves may also be treated with glycerine.

Picking

Since the aim is to replace the moisture in the plant with glycerine, it is vital to pick plants before the sap begins to leave the stems. Very young foliage does not take up moisture very readily, so pick mature green foliage, but not foliage which has

A magnificent array of dried flowers and foliage: the outline material is glycerined beech leaves, and sand-dried delphiniums, air-dried bachelor's buttons and Alchemilla mollis comprise the filling materials.

Hillier and Hilton

begun to turn colour in the autumn, as this indicates that the sap has stopped flowing and the stem will not therefore be able to absorb the preserving solution.

Some experts maintain that any length of stem can be used, even branches up to two metres (six feet) in length, but it is probably wise to use shorter branches in the beginning—up to one metre (three feet)—since a very long branch may make it difficult for glycerine to reach the tip, and consequently it may wilt.

However, it is always well worth experimenting with different lengths of branches according to your requirements. There is nothing to lose apart from a quantity of glycerine and a little of your own time.

Method

It is best to condition branches in deep water for several hours so that they are as full of water as possible. Wash the leaves if they are dirty and remove any damaged or unwanted foliage, in order to avoid wasting glycerine.

Woody stems should be treated as described in chapter three—that is, they should be scraped and crushed or split—to ensure maximum absorption of glycerine.

Glycerine preparation. Glycerine must be diluted as it is too viscous to be absorbed easily on its own. (Eventually, the water in the solution evaporates from the plant, leaving the glycerine behind.)

There is some controversy about the exact proportions of glycerine to water to use, but one part glycerine to two parts water should be strong enough for most foliage. Equal parts of each may be necessary for tougher leaves such as laurel and aspidistra.

Use water that is nearly boiling, as hot fluid travels more quickly up the stem. Stir the mixture well as glycerine has a tendency to sink to the bottom.

Immersion. Place stem ends in about 10–15 centimetres (4–6 inches) of the solution and leave in a cool, dark, dry place until all the leaves have changed colour. Inspect them frequently to see how things are going and whether the glycerine solution needs topping up.

Small leaves. Some small leaves which absorb the solution slowly may be totally immersed in glycerine solution in a shallow dish, to speed up the process. As soon as they turn colour, gently wash them free of excess solution and let them dry on blotting paper. Such leaves include ivy, lily of the valley, bergenia and *Fatsia japonica*.

Timing. The time it takes for the glycerine to become absorbed depends on the type of plant material concerned. In general, the tougher the leaf, the longer it takes. The leaves of eucalyptus and beech only take a week, while tougher leaves, such as aspidistra, camellia and laurel may take up to six or even ten weeks. It is possible to speed up the process with such leaves by coating them with the solution, applied with cotton wool, before standing their stems in it.

The plant material is ready when the leaves have completely changed colour—it is often possible to see the progress of the glycerine as the colour changes from green to brown. The undersides of the leaves should be oily.

Do not leave the material standing in the solution for too long. The solution should not be allowed to start dripping off the ends of the leaves, or to appear in oily beads on the surface of the leaves. Leaves which are left for too long may even become mildewed so it is wise to maintain a regular check on progress every so often.

Wipe leaves and stem ends with cotton wool or a paper tissue on removal, both to discourage mildew and to prevent grease marks on wallpaper if the plants are to be arranged at once. If leaves seem to wither after their removal from the glycerine, hang them upside down for a few days so that the glycerine moves to the very tips.

Re-use. Glycerine solution may be re-used. Mould sometimes grows in the solution if it is kept for a long time, but this can be discouraged with a quarter of a teaspoon of a mild disinfectant to half a litre (one pint) of the solution.

Mementos of the family life of Queen Victoria are displayed on a fabric-draped table. The sepia tones of the early photographs, and the pink and brown pattern of the cloth are echoed in the pale, papery petals of dried hydrangeas. Because of their subtle tones and delicate, yet massed shape, dried hydrangeas are especially popular.

THE VICTORIAN
SOCIETY
ANNUAL 1969-70

Pressing

The uses of pressed flowers and plants as foliage in dried arrangements and as pressed flower collages and pictures are described further on in this chapter. The preparation of materials is described here.

Choosing the material

Pressing is only suitable for fairly flat plant material such as leaves, ferns, grasses, bracken and wild flowers. Thin, flat flowers with very fine tissue such as violets and daisies and many wild flowers can be pressed successfully. However, plants with rigid tissue or fleshy succulents with a high moisture content cannot. Also unsuitable are flowers with hard, heavy centres which prevent their petals from being pressed properly. Petals can be pressed separately, however, and then reassembled for a pressed flower picture using a smaller flower for a centre, or a flatter centre from another flower to make up the design.

Pressed flower pictures will need fairly small flowers and leaves unless the aim is a large, ambitious project. Larger flower heads such as roses and daffodils can be pulled apart, however, and each petal pressed separately, and those such as delphiniums and hydrangeas can be divided into individual florets before pressing.

For pictures, choose thin stalks such as primrose, clematis and buttercup. If any thicker stalks are needed, choose soft ones because hard stems do not press well.

Colour retention. In general, yellow and orange flowers such as buttercups, celandine and montbretia keep their colour the best when pressed. Blue remains in delphiniums and lobelias, but not so well in other flowers. White usually turns beige but is retained in cow parsley (Queen Anne's lace), daisies, astrantias and hellebores. Roses do not keep their colour well but tend to turn a cream colour, while deep red ones go brown. This does not necessarily mean that roses should not be pressed

for flower pictures; interesting use can be made of these soft, muted shades.

As for leaves, some retain their colour, particularly grey ones and autumn leaves which have already turned brown. Young green leaves tend to change colour: young maple, for example, goes pale green or yellow; young ash turns black; and ivy tends to go brown.

Picking

As always, plants should be in the peak of condition when picked. They should be dry and clean, so any dirt should be cleaned off gently with a damp tissue, and surplus damp removed on blotting paper. Always press plants immediately after picking them.

The creative uses of pressed plants and flowers are considerable. Delicate borders for pictures can be made, as can imaginative collages like the one shown here which includes a floral house, garden and trees.

How to press

Plant material can be pressed in a flower press or in a heavy book (some foliage can be pressed with an iron and this is described later on). The essential thing is to arrange flowers between layers of blotting paper so that different parts do not touch each other. If the leaves or petals of one overlap, place a small piece of tissue paper between the two layers.

Use a small, soft paint-brush to arrange delicate material so that it is not torn or bruised with careless handling.

Curve some stems slightly, using adhesive tape if necessary.

(If you use a book, bear in mind that the process will tend to put strain on the spine and stain the paper, so choose something valueless such as an old telephone directory.)

If the centre of a flower is hard, press it down firmly with your thumb. Flowers with exceptionally hard, fat centres, or those with a difficult shape such as roses and tulips, should be dismantled and their petals arranged separately. Three-dimensional flowers such as daffodils and narcissi can be cut into two with scissors and pressed in two halves, thus giving two flowers—side views—for a picture. Divide up sprays and clusters such as delphiniums and hydrangeas into individual florets.

Timing. Pressed material should be left in the press or book for at least six weeks in a warm, dry place. The time depends on the temperature of the room and the material in question.

If the plants are very moist and fleshy, it may be necessary to change the blotting paper after 24 hours or so, and perhaps again after another 48 hours, as the blotting paper might otherwise become damp or even mouldy. If a flower press is being used, tighten the wing nuts regularly (but gently) for the first ten days, as the material settles.

Some people advocate pressing plant material for pictures, especially flowers, for at least three months and preferably for as long as a year, because the longer it is left the thinner it becomes, and the less likely the colours are to fade when they are exposed to light. The problem here, if you are using a flower press, is that the same flowers will monopolize the press for a long time. One solution is to move the plants from the press to a heavy book after a few weeks and to leave them there until

needed. It is a good idea to start at the back of the book and work towards the front so that the plants are not disturbed as the book is filled up.

It is also a good idea to arrange material according to type, colour, and so on, and to label pages accordingly with a book mark, perhaps also giving the date of pressing. Keep the book tightly closed with an elastic band and store it in a dry place.

Pressing with an Iron

Some foliage can be pressed quickly with a domestic iron, but the results do not last as long as with the slower method of pressing.

Method

Place the leaf between sheets of newspaper or blotting paper and press firmly with the iron set at 'wool' for up to five minutes, depending on the thickness of the leaf. Lift off the top piece of paper every now and again during the procedure to release steam. The leaf may flop at first but should become stiff as it dries.

Complete the pressing by placing the leaves under a carpet for about a week or, if you are really in a hurry, under a weight in the airing cupboard overnight. These leaves usually turn a dull green or brown colour.

Globe artichokes, varnished gourds, hydrangeas, magnolia leaves, iris seed-pods, millet, onion heads and hops, wired on a central support, make this elaborate dried display. Below: two ways to press.

David Hicks

Storage

When fresh flowers are in the garden it is often a good idea to replace preserved displays with fresh ones, and to store the preserved material until the following autumn.

Ideally, a special place which can be devoted to storing preserved material is needed—a corner in a cool, airy, dry outhouse, or a garage or an attic, for example. Cleanliness is of great importance if the plants are not to become dusty, but damp is the greatest enemy of all: it causes mildew, wilting and discoloration.

If plant material is preserved on a large scale, it is vital to label the contents of boxes so that you can find things easily when it comes to designing arrangements.

Special florist's boxes with lids are perfect but it is equally possible to use shoe boxes and wine or spirit cartons.

Spread clear polythene or sheets of paper over boxes without lids to stop dust settling on the contents. All lids should have air holes.

Some fragile flower heads can be stored on wires in jars of sand or in dry foam, though it is obviously more difficult to keep them free of dust.

Air-dried material. Store in cardboard boxes, jars of sand, or in dry foam, or hang upside down in bunches.

Pressed flowers and leaves. Store in a book or between sheets of blotting paper under a weight.

Desiccated material. Store in a dark place such as a covered box or tin, with a few grains of desiccant to ward off damp. Flowers can also be wired and stuck into dry foam which will prevent crushing.

Dry-cleaning fluid may be used if flowers become dirty.

Glycerined material. Store in boxes or upright in containers. Glycerined leaves are supple and tough and there is no need for careful packing, as they are not easily crushed.

Never store glycerined plants in polythene bags or they will become mildewed.

If material gets dirty, it may be washed in water and a little detergent, and should then be dried thoroughly on blotting paper.

Dried gypsophila makes a simple yet imposing tree-like background for this papier-mâché Royal family.

Arranging

The principles of design are much the same when arranging preserved flowers and foliage as they are where fresh flowers are concerned. The only major difference is that, since there is less variety and intensity of colour, more attention must be paid to variations in form and texture.

Colour and texture

Colour and texture are major elements of the flower arranger's art and it is therefore very important to consider the effects of preserving on both the natural colour and the 'feel' of different flowers and plants. These vary according to the plant and, to some degree, on the type of preservative used.

While dessicant-dried flowers tend to retain their original colours, air-dried flowers, as a rule, become more subdued in tone and many plants, such as grasses and some hydrangeas, turn shades of soft brown, beige or pale cream. The everlasting sandflowers, however, keep their rich hues of pink, cream, yellow and bronze.

Remember that glycerined leaves always change colour, generally turning 'autumnal' browns, purples and faded greens.

Nearly all preserved plants undergo changes in texture, becoming stiff or crinkly if dried, leathery if glycerined, and these qualities also influence the appearance of the arrangement. But, rather than reducing design potential, preserved materials widen it, putting a new range of tints and textures at the flower arranger's fingertips.

Mechanics

The mechanics of arranging are only very slightly different from those used with fresh material.

Wires. Stems tend to be stiff and brittle (glycerined material being an exception) and many flower and seed heads need to be wired. Both dried stems and wires need slightly different treatment from fresh, pliable stems.

Stub wires have already been discussed in chapter four and, to some extent, in this section. The thicker wires such as 0.90 mm and 0.71 mm (20 and 22 gauge) are the most useful for preserved plant material, but if it is very delicate foliage, a much finer stub wire should be used. The wiring of dried flower heads has already been described

on page 170. Leaves can be wired by pushing a stub wire through the base of the leaf, bending the wire double, and binding it together with fine reel wire or fuse wire. If the leaf is floppy and needs some support, lay a stub wire across the back of the leaf and hold it in place with transparent glue such as UHU, or with clear adhesive tape. As in the case of fresh plant material, the hollow stem of a preserved flower can be reinforced by pushing a stub wire up through the centre of the stalk.

Binding tape such as gutta-percha is especially useful for preparing dried plant material, as it can be used to cover false stems. This adhesive tape can be bought in a variety of colours but an inconspicuous brown or beige is obviously most suited to dried arrangements.

To cover a wire stem, begin binding at the top of the stalk. Hold the wire just below the flower head between the forefinger and thumb of one hand, and start winding the tape with the other hand. Work tightly and at a slight downward angle. (See illustration on page 51.)

Support. Stems may be supported in plastic, water-retaining foam, used dry, or special foam made of a heavier consistency, which is sold specifically for dried arrangements. Both these need to be firmly fixed in the container, and a special pinholder with a few widely-spaced prongs may be bought for this purpose. Alternatively, it is possible to obtain from florists a small saucer which is already fitted with needles or a plastic ring to anchor a piece of foam (see page 46).

A dried arrangement can also be supported in a vase filled with sand or small pebbles. For a permanent arrangement, plaster of Paris provides a heavy, stable base.

Glycerined material can be supported in exactly the same way as fresh plant material.

Large-holed chicken wire can also be used to support flowers. In rather tall arrangements where masses of short flowers and foliage are used, the wire should be crumpled into a mound which rises considerably higher than the container. The flowers can then be stuck into the mesh or tied to it with silver reel wire. In such arrangements, it is best to begin at the top and work downwards, covering all sides as you go. An example of this type of arrangement is shown overleaf.

Containers

The same containers as those for fresh flowers can often be used, although glass vases are best avoided since dried stems tend not to be very attractive, and false stems should be as invisible as possible.

As water is not used to weigh down the container, it is best to use stable containers with heavy bases and low centres of gravity, and it may be necessary to weigh them down further with sand or pebbles. Containers such as baskets, which, without a liner, would not be possible for fresh flowers, may also be used. Or, containers can be dispensed with altogether.

Mixed fresh and dried plants

It is possible to combine both types of material in an arrangement but, of course, water will be needed to keep fresh flowers fresh, so dried material must be protected. To do this, seal dried stem ends with a thick layer of varnish, nail varnish or sealing wax. Alternatively, dried stems can be grouped in a separate dry container within the one holding water, or vice versa. Dried stems may also be protected in a polythene bag within the container.

The muted colours of these dried hydrangeas add a suggestion of warmth to the cool, elegant setting.

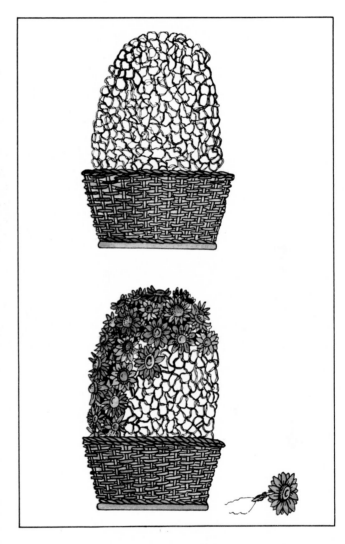

This delightful example of air-dried flowers by
Kenneth Turner shows how spring-like dried
materials can be. The wicker basket adds to the effect.

   The arrangement is made by crumpling chicken
wire in a container so that it makes a tall mound, as
shown.

   Each flower is wired with silver reel wire and tied
to the mesh of the chicken wire. The arranger should
begin at the top and work in a downward spiral.

Kenneth Turner

These two pictures show the importance of careful styling which can transform a bundle of unexciting grasses, picked on a country walk, into an attractive design of soft, warm colours and subtle tonal relationships. A balance of length and texture is as crucial to the overall effect as is consideration of colour. In the picture above, the grasses have just been arranged while fresh, and there is water in the vase. As this evaporates the grasses begin to dry, turning the golden colour shown opposite.

David Hicks

An opulent and very colourful arrangement of dried
flowers, using a barrel for the container, is shown
above. The materials are delphiniums, Alchemilla,
larkspur, wild grasses, onion heads, peonies,
artichokes, Stacyss, Rodinthus, Acarolium, oak
leaves, bracken, Echnopisis and Ambia. The
flowers are supported in meshed chicken wire.
Opposite: a miniature basket of dried flowers makes
a delicate posy.

David Hicks

Two dried displays are shown here: both concentrate
on brown wintry colouring for their effect, and are
composed mainly of leaves, grasses and foodstuffs.
Above, a huge arrangement for a pedestal includes
bulrushes, pampas grass, box, hemlock and oak
leaves. The example opposite is evocative of arable
fields in the countryside. It contains maize, seed-pods,
beans, bay leaves, dried fungus, poppy heads, onion
heads, Alchemilla and lichen. The maize husks are
pulled outward to form a flower and to create a focal
point along with the spray of beans.

Kenneth Turner

This eye-deceiving arrangement of dahlias in a copper
bowl is composed entirely of dried materials.
Glycerined beech leaves are put in first to form the
outline of the shape—in this case, domed—then the
dahlias, dried in sand and wired on long false stems,
are studded at regular intervals round the leaves.
The base of the arrangement is floral foam. The
subdued shade of glycerined beech and the russet and
gold tones of the dahlias blend well in their
predominantly brown surroundings and, while
appearing fresh, create an autumnal mood in keeping
with the season in which preserved flowers are most
often used.

Hillier and Hilton

The world of Alice in Wonderland is evoked by the fanciful scene opposite. The mysterious mushroom-shaped tree appears firmly rooted in its wicker basket and, although very large, is dwarfed by wispy overhanging grasses and giant hogweed. All are ordinary, natural materials which owe their appearance to the air-drying process and, in the case of the mushroom tree, to the imagination of its creator, Kenneth Turner. It is in fact made of moss-covered chicken wire by the process illustrated.

First a tree limb is 'planted' in a pot of plaster of Paris, then a huge ball of crumpled chicken wire is placed on top of the limb, and secured. This is covered by sack moss to form a base for the bunn moss which is pinned on in sections, while still moist. The 'tree' is allowed to dry out and it is placed in a basket. The plaster of Paris is hidden by a layer of dried grass. Such a tree could be made on a much smaller scale, similar to that of the rose tree shown on page 122, for example.

Pressed Flower Pictures

Pressed flower pictures are flower arrangements and they demand the same artistic considerations of colour, shape, texture and design as do conventional arrangements. However, since flower pictures are two-dimensional, the results of applying these principles will be quite different.

Equipment

As well as the pressed plants, art paper or thick card is needed for a background (silk or velvet can be used as well). Heavy cardboard or hardboard is usually necessary for a backing, and glass. All three should be cut to the same size. Fabric should be stretched over card. It is best to choose a frame first and then cut card, hardboard and glass to fit the frame, or it can simply be held together with mirror clips.

A latex-based adhesive such as Copydex is needed for sticking the plants in place. The advantage of a latex-based adhesive is that it does not show through the plant and it can be removed without leaving a mark.

Scissors are essential for trimming, and a thin knife, tweezers and a soft paintbrush are all useful to position delicate material.

Making the picture

It is a good idea to plan the design on paper beforehand, to avoid rearranging fragile plant material over and over again. Lift the plant material and place it in position with a thin knife or tweezers, or push it into place with a paintbrush. Handle it as little as possible.

These delightful pressed flower pictures show the wide variety of flowers and leaves that can be used. The picture below, for example, is made up of montbretia, lady's bedstraw, red encra, daisies, carrot leaves, Californian poppy, pansies and a wild geranium leaf.

Sue Frankland

Made-up Flowers

Artificial flowers may be made up from parts of preserved material. For example, several honesty seed pods may be wired individually, using fine reel wire, and grouped together to form flower petals. Then a seed head or a small dried flower may be wired and added as a flower centre. Bind the wires together with the reel wire or twist them together and cover stem with floral tape. (See chapter four for information on using reel wire and floral tape.)

The same method may be applied to leaves. Wire several brown, glycerined leaves, for example, and add a tiny pine cone for a centre.

There is no end to the possible combinations of leaves, seed heads and flowers. A small, brightly coloured feather might be added here and there to add a startling flash of brilliance to a design.

The four 'flowers' used in the arrangement shown are made as follows:

Sprays of 'lilies'. These are glycerined magnolia leaves wrapped round ears of wheat and bound together with floral tape. A stub wire is bound to the natural stem to give support and flexibility. Three 'lilies' are bound together with floral tape to make a spray.

Green 'daisies'. Six magnolia leaves are wired to an achillia spray one at a time with silver reel wire. Care is needed to avoid tearing the leaves. The stem is bound with floral tape.

The 'teazel flowers' are made in the same way as the 'daisies' just described but their petals are of glycerined beech leaves.

'Roses'. These fanciful creations are composed of a fir-cone and honesty. The scaly covering and seed must be removed from the honesty seed cases so that their flat, satin shapes are revealed. The seed cases must also be removed from their stems. The fir-cone is attached to a stub wire as illustrated and a general-purpose glue such as UHU is inserted between the scales. The honesty is stuck on using the smallest size first, and working from the top of the fir-cone downwards. Finally, the flower stem is covered with floral tape.

Far right: this simple arrangement of 'flowers' made up from easily obtainable materials which have been reassembled, as a slightly exotic flavour.

A glycerined magnolia leaf and an ear of wheat.

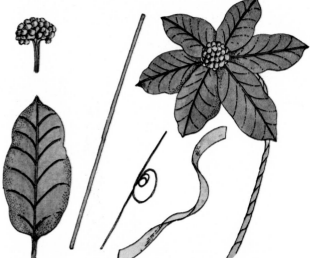

A glycerined magnolia leaf and an achillea spray.

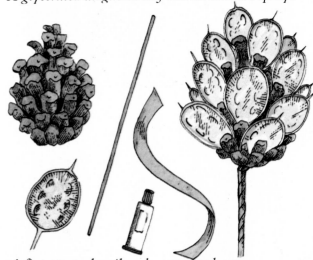

A fir-cone and a silver honesty seed-case.

Flower Guide

In this A-to-Z list the generic name is followed by any common name, plant type, growing season, estimated lifespan in water, colours, and any useful comments.★

Achillea
Yarrow
Herbaceous perennial
Summer
1 week
Yellow, white and red
Yellow dries well

Agapanthus
African lily
Perennial
Late summer, autumn
1 week
Umbels of blue and
    blue violet
Seed heads dry well

Alchemilla mollis
Lady's mantle
Herbaceous perennial
Mid-summer
1 week
Tiny lime green flowers
Pale green pleated leaves

Alstroemeria
Peruvian lily
Herbaceous perennial
Summer
1–2 weeks
White, pink, mauve,
    red, yellow orange

Anaphalis
Pearl everlasting
Herbaceous perennial
Summer
1 week
White
Dries well

Anemone
Windflower
Herbaceous perennial
Early spring; summer
    and autumn
1 week
Various including blue
Prefer cool

Aquilegia
Columbine
Herbaceous perennial
Early summer
1 week
White, pink, blue,
    mauve, yellow

Aster
*Michaelmas daisy; New
    York Aster*
Herbaceous perennial
Late summer and
    autumn
10 days
Pinks and mauve,
    daisy-like flowers

Astrantia
Masterwort
Herbaceous perennial
Mid summer
1 week
Grey, mauve, starry
    flowers

★ *The flowers are not drawn to scale.*

Bergenia
Herbaceous perennial
Early spring
5 days
Purple pink, pink, pale
    pink
Useful evergreen leaves

Clematis
Virgin's bower
Climber
Late spring, summer,
    autumn
White, pink, violet,
    purple stars
Boil or singe

Calendula officinalis
Pot marigold
Annual
Late spring to autumn
2 weeks
Yellow, orange, daisy-
    like flowers
Remove foliage below
    water level

Convallaria majalis
Lily of the valley
Herbaceous perennial
Spring
3–4 days
White bells
Fragrant

Callistephus
China aster
Annual
Mid summer to autumn
10 days
White, pink, red, purple
Dense, daisy-like
    flowers

Coreopsis
Tickseed
Hardy annual;
    herbaceous perennial
Mid- and late summer
1 week
Yellow-gold, daisy-like
Some with red
    centres

Centaurea cyanus
Cornflower
Annual
Summer
1 week
White, pink, red,
    purple, blue

Cornus
Cornel, dogwood
Tree, shrub
Spring and summer
5 days
White or pink bracts
Split stem; can force

Chrysanthemum
Incl. Shasta daisy
Annual; herbaceous
    perennial
Summer and autumn
2 weeks
Various, not blue or
    purple
Scrape and remove
    foliage below water
    level

Dahlia
Tuber
Summer and autumn
5 days
Various, not blue and
    purple
Below water cut at
    slant; split stem
    between joints

Delphinium
Annual; herbaceous
  perennial
Summer
1 week
White, blue, mauve,
  cream, red-orange

Erigeron
Fleabane
Perennial
Summer
1 week
Yellow, mauve, blue-
  mauve

Dianthus barbatus
Sweet William
Perennial
Early summer
10 days
White, pink, red
Cut on slant above
  joint

Eryngium
Sea holly
Herbaceous perennial
Mid- and late summer
1 week
Blue teasel-like head of
  tiny flowers
  with a collar of
  spiny bracts
Dries well

**Dianthus
caryophyllus**
Carnation; Gillyflower
Perennial
Summer
10 days
White, cream, apricot,
  pink, red, crimson
Cut on slant above joint

**Eschscholtzia
californica**
Californian poppy
Annual
Summer and autumn
1 week
Cream, yellow, orange,
  pink, crimson
Cut in bud

Digitalis
Foxglove
Biennial and perennial
Summer
1 week
White, mauve, pink,
  purple, yellow,
  apricot
Spire of bells

Euphorbia
Spurge
Incl. herbaceous
Spring, summer
2 weeks
Lime green, green-
  maroon
Bracts petal-like,
  highly coloured
Reds and orange

Echinops
Globe thistle
Herbaceous biennial
  and perennial
Mid-summer
2 weeks
Blue globular head of
  flowers
Dries well

Forsythia
Golden bells
Shrub
Early spring
5 days
Yellow

Freesia
Bulb
Summer
5 days
Cream, yellow, pink,
  mauve
Remove individual
  blooms as they die

Hamamelis mollis
Witch hazel
Shrub
Winter
2 weeks
Yellow spidery,
  fragrant
Hammer stems

Gaillardia
Blanket flower
Annual; perennial
Summer and autumn
1 week
Yellow, orange-red,
  crimson

Helleborus
Hardy perennial
Winter
2 weeks
White, pink, dusky
  mauve, pale green
Make a cut down the
  length of the stem

Garrya elliptica
Evergreen shrub
Winter
10 days
Long grey-green
  catkins
Catkins of male plant
  more ornamental

Hosta
Funkia
Herbaceous perennial
Summer
5 days
Lilac, white, trumpet-
  shaped
Leaves much prized

Gladiolus
Sword lily
Bulb
Summer
10 days
Cream, yellow, apricot,
  bronze, crimson,
  scarlet, lavender and
  pale green
Remove individual
  blooms as they die

Hydrangea
Shrub
Summer
1 week
Cream, pink, red, blue
  of small massed flowers,
Peel and split stem,
  boil
Immerse and arrange in
  luke-warm water

Gypsophila
Baby's breath
Annual; perennial
Summer
1 week
White, pink, tiny star-
  like flowers
G. paniculata dries

Iris
Flag
Early summer
1 week
White, yellow, apricot,
  violet, purple, bronze
Remove dead flowers,
  buds continue to
  open

Jasminum nudiflorum
Jasmine
Shrub
Winter
5 days
Bright yellow
Can cut in tight bud in
    frost

Narcissus
Daffodil; jonquil
Bulb
Early spring
1 week
White, cream, yellow
Cut as buds show colour
Wipe off sap before
    putting in water

Lathyrus
*Sweet pea; everlasting
    pea*
Annual; herbaceous
    perennial
Summer, early autumn
1 week
White, pink, mauve,
    purple, cream,
    orange, scarlet

Nerine bowdenii
Bulb
Late summer
1 week
Sugar-pink umbel

Lilium
Lily
Bulb
Summer, early autumn
1 week
White, pink, red,
    yellow, orange,
    scarlet

Nicotiana
Tobacco plant
Annual; herbaceous
    perennial
Summer and autumn
4–5 days
White, yellow-green,
    pink, red, mauve,
    crimson
White flowers are
    fragrant

Magnolia
Tree and shrub
Spring and summer
1 week
White, rose-purple,
    red-purple
Cut in advanced bud;
    boil

Nigella damascena
Love-in-a-mist
Annual
Summer
1 week
White, clue, pink,
    mauve
Feathery foliage, good
    seed pods

Mathiola
Stock; Brompton stock
Annual; biennial;
    perennial herbaceous
Summer
5 days
Cream, pink mauve,
    purple, crimson,
    yellow
Heavy scent

**Ornithogalum
umbellatum**
Star of Bethlehem
Bulb
Early summer
2 weeks
White with green
Cut in bud; remove
    dried flowers;
    change water

Paeonia
Peony
Herbaceous perennial
  and shrub
Late spring and
  summer
1 week
White, pale cream, red
  pink, mauve, yellow,
Cut in bud; boil

Phlox
Herbaceous perennial
Summer
1 week
White, pink, red, purple
Pick in bud; cut above
  joint

Papaver orientale
Oriental poppy
Perennial
Late spring, early
  summer
4 days
Scarlet, pinks, orange,
  white
Cut before it opens
Singe and soak

Phygelius capensis
Cape fuchsia
Shrub
Late summer, autumn
5 days
Orange-scarlet panicles
Split stems

Pelargonium
Geranium
Sub shrub
Early summer to
  autumn
1 week
White, pink, mauve,
  crimson, maroon,
  scarlet

**Platycodon
grandiflorum**
Balloon flower
Herbaceous perennial
Summer
1 week
White, pink, blue
Balloon-shaped in
  bud, it opens to
  star-like flower

Penstemon
Herbaceous perennial
Summer
5 days
Pink, mauve, crimson,
  blue, red, purple,
  green

**Polygonatum
multiflorum**
Solomon's seal
Herbaceous perennial
Summer
1 week
White with green
  markings
Graceful stems, clusters
  of tubular flowers

Philadelphus
Mock orange
Shrub
Summer
1 week
White, very fragrant
Split stems

Primula
Primrose
Hardy and half-hardy
  perennial
Spring
4 days
Various colours

211

Prunus
Ornamental cherry
Tree and shrub
Early spring
5 days
White, yellow, pink
Boil

Romneya
California tree poppy
Herbaceous perennial
Late summer and
    autumn
5 days
Papery white with bold
    yellow centre
Cut with buds half
    open; singe

Pyracantha
Firethorn
Evergreen shrub
Summer
4 days
Clusters of tiny, creamy
    white flowers
Berries in bright yellow,
    orange, red

Rosa
Rose
Perennial
Summer, autumn
5 days
Various colours
Hammer stems

Pyrethrum
Herbaceous perennial
Summer
1 week
White, pink, carmine,
    red

Rudbeckia
*Coneflower. Black-eyed
    Susan*
Annual; herbaceous
    perennial
Late summer
10 days
Yellow, yellow and red
    with black eye.

Ranunculus
Buttercup
Annual; herbaceous
    perennial
Spring, summer
10 days
White, yellow, pink,
    red, orange

Scabiosa
*Scabious; Pincushion
    flower*
Annual; herbaceous
    perennial
Summer
10 days
Blue, mauve, pink,
    crimson, white

Rhododendron
Evergreen tree and
    shrub
Spring and summer
1 week
White, pink, crimson,
    violet, purple, apricot
Boil

Schizostylis
Perennial
Autumn
1 week
White, pink, red

Sedum
Annual; perennial
Mid-summer, early
    autumn
10 days
Pink

Tropaeolum majus
Nasturtium
Annual
Summer
4 days
Yellow orange scarlet,
    pink, crimson

**Symphoricarpos
rivularis**
Snowberry
Shrub
Summer
Pink
Large white fruits in
    autumn
Strip off foliage
Berries last weeks

Tulipa
Tulip
Bulb
Late spring
1 week
White, pink, red,
    crimson-purple,
    cream, yellow,
    orange, scarlet

Syringa
Lilac
Small tree and shrub
Late spring
1 week
White, pale yellow,
    pink, violet, purple
Strip off leaves
Can boil

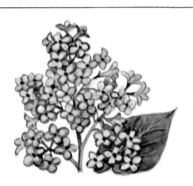

Viola
Pansy
Annual; perennial
Summer
4 days
Various, including blue
    and deep purple

Tagetes
*African and French
    marigold*
Annual; herbaceous
    perennial
Mid- and late summer
1 week
Yellow, gold, red
Scrape, strip off leaves
    below water level

Weigela florida
Shrub
Early summer
5 days
Pale pink
Green, variegated or
    purple foliage
Soak

Trollius
Globe flower
Herbaceous perennial
Summer
10 days
Yellow, buttercup-like
Cut as colour shows
Deep water

Zinnia
Youth-and-old-age
Annual; perennial
Summer, autumn
2 weeks
Various, not blue
Cut when just opened,
    above leaf joint
Remove excess foliage
    and spray

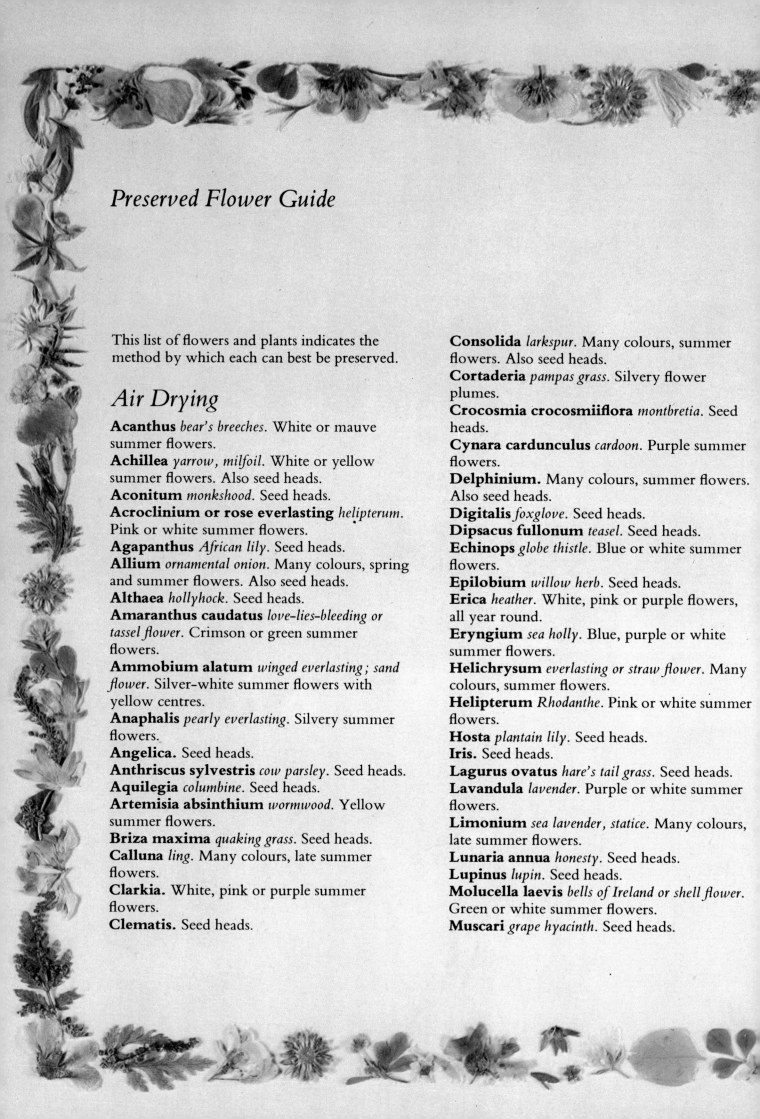

Preserved Flower Guide

This list of flowers and plants indicates the method by which each can best be preserved.

Air Drying

Acanthus *bear's breeches*. White or mauve summer flowers.

Achillea *yarrow, milfoil*. White or yellow summer flowers. Also seed heads.

Aconitum *monkshood*. Seed heads.

Acroclinium or rose everlasting *helipterum*. Pink or white summer flowers.

Agapanthus *African lily*. Seed heads.

Allium *ornamental onion*. Many colours, spring and summer flowers. Also seed heads.

Althaea *hollyhock*. Seed heads.

Amaranthus caudatus *love-lies-bleeding or tassel flower*. Crimson or green summer flowers.

Ammobium alatum *winged everlasting; sand flower*. Silver-white summer flowers with yellow centres.

Anaphalis *pearly everlasting*. Silvery summer flowers.

Angelica. Seed heads.

Anthriscus sylvestris *cow parsley*. Seed heads.

Aquilegia *columbine*. Seed heads.

Artemisia absinthium *wormwood*. Yellow summer flowers.

Briza maxima *quaking grass*. Seed heads.

Calluna *ling*. Many colours, late summer flowers.

Clarkia. White, pink or purple summer flowers.

Clematis. Seed heads.

Consolida *larkspur*. Many colours, summer flowers. Also seed heads.

Cortaderia *pampas grass*. Silvery flower plumes.

Crocosmia crocosmiiflora *montbretia*. Seed heads.

Cynara cardunculus *cardoon*. Purple summer flowers.

Delphinium. Many colours, summer flowers. Also seed heads.

Digitalis *foxglove*. Seed heads.

Dipsacus fullonum *teasel*. Seed heads.

Echinops *globe thistle*. Blue or white summer flowers.

Epilobium *willow herb*. Seed heads.

Erica *heather*. White, pink or purple flowers, all year round.

Eryngium *sea holly*. Blue, purple or white summer flowers.

Helichrysum *everlasting or straw flower*. Many colours, summer flowers.

Helipterum *Rhodanthe*. Pink or white summer flowers.

Hosta *plantain lily*. Seed heads.

Iris. Seed heads.

Lagurus ovatus *hare's tail grass*. Seed heads.

Lavandula *lavender*. Purple or white summer flowers.

Limonium *sea lavender, statice*. Many colours, late summer flowers.

Lunaria annua *honesty*. Seed heads.

Lupinus *lupin*. Seed heads.

Molucella laevis *bells of Ireland or shell flower*. Green or white summer flowers.

Muscari *grape hyacinth*. Seed heads.

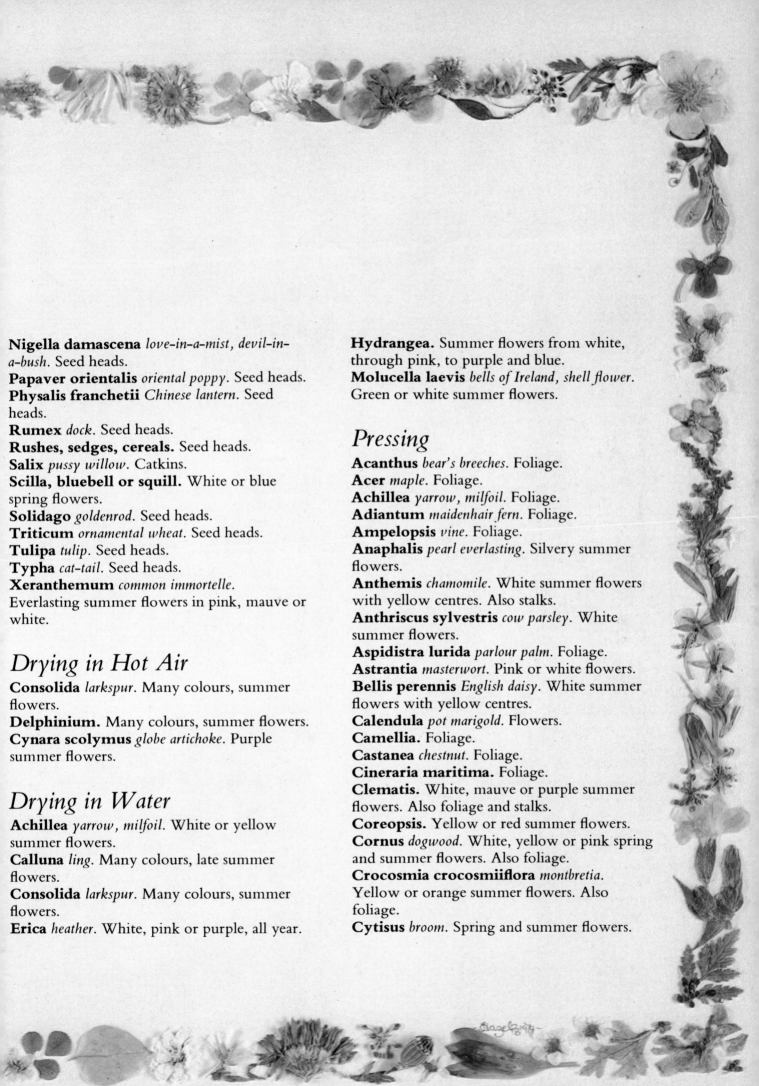

Nigella damascena *love-in-a-mist, devil-in-a-bush*. Seed heads.
Papaver orientalis *oriental poppy*. Seed heads.
Physalis franchetii *Chinese lantern*. Seed heads.
Rumex *dock*. Seed heads.
Rushes, sedges, cereals. Seed heads.
Salix *pussy willow*. Catkins.
Scilla, bluebell or squill. White or blue spring flowers.
Solidago *goldenrod*. Seed heads.
Triticum *ornamental wheat*. Seed heads.
Tulipa *tulip*. Seed heads.
Typha *cat-tail*. Seed heads.
Xeranthemum *common immortelle*. Everlasting summer flowers in pink, mauve or white.

Drying in Hot Air

Consolida *larkspur*. Many colours, summer flowers.
Delphinium. Many colours, summer flowers.
Cynara scolymus *globe artichoke*. Purple summer flowers.

Drying in Water

Achillea *yarrow, milfoil*. White or yellow summer flowers.
Calluna *ling*. Many colours, late summer flowers.
Consolida *larkspur*. Many colours, summer flowers.
Erica *heather*. White, pink or purple, all year.

Hydrangea. Summer flowers from white, through pink, to purple and blue.
Molucella laevis *bells of Ireland, shell flower*. Green or white summer flowers.

Pressing

Acanthus *bear's breeches*. Foliage.
Acer *maple*. Foliage.
Achillea *yarrow, milfoil*. Foliage.
Adiantum *maidenhair fern*. Foliage.
Ampelopsis *vine*. Foliage.
Anaphalis *pearl everlasting*. Silvery summer flowers.
Anthemis *chamomile*. White summer flowers with yellow centres. Also stalks.
Anthriscus sylvestris *cow parsley*. White summer flowers.
Aspidistra lurida *parlour palm*. Foliage.
Astrantia *masterwort*. Pink or white flowers.
Bellis perennis *English daisy*. White summer flowers with yellow centres.
Calendula *pot marigold*. Flowers.
Camellia. Foliage.
Castanea *chestnut*. Foliage.
Cineraria maritima. Foliage.
Clematis. White, mauve or purple summer flowers. Also foliage and stalks.
Coreopsis. Yellow or red summer flowers.
Cornus *dogwood*. White, yellow or pink spring and summer flowers. Also foliage.
Crocosmia crocosmiiflora *montbretia*. Yellow or orange summer flowers. Also foliage.
Cytisus *broom*. Spring and summer flowers.

Daffodil. Yellow spring flowers.
Delphinium. Many colours, summer flowers. Also foliage.
Fagus *beech*. Foliage.
Ferns. All varieties. Foliage.
Fraxinus *ash*. Foliage.
Gladiolus. Foliage.
Grasses. All flatter varieties. Foliage.
Hedera *ivy*. Foliage.
Helleborus *Christmas and Lenten rose*. White, dark red or green winter and spring flowers. Also foliage.
Helipterum *everlasting or rhodanthe*. Pink or white summer flowers.
Hydrangea. Summer flowers from white, through pink, to purple and blue.
Iris. Foliage.
Laburnum *golden chain*. Yellow spring and early summer flowers.
Laurus *Grecian laurel, sweet bay, bay*. Foliage.
Lobelia. Blue or white summer flowers.
Lonicera *honeysuckle*. Foliage.
Lunaria annua *honesty*. Purple summer flowers.
Narcissus. White or yellow summer flowers.
Nicotiana *tobacco plant*. White, pink or green summer flowers.
Paeonia *peony*. Foliage.
Papaver nudicaule *Iceland poppy*. Many colours, summer flowers.
Parthenocissus *Virginia creeper*. Foliage.
Pelargonium *horseshoe geranium*. Foliage.
Polyanthus *polyanthus primrose*. Many colours, spring flowers.
Populus tremula *aspen*. Foliage.

Primula *primrose*. Many colours, spring flowers. Also stalks.
Prunus *cherry, plum, peach*. Foliage.
Quercus *oak*. Foliage.
Ranunculus *buttercup*. Yellow summer flowers. Also stalks.
Ranunculus ficaria *celandine*. Yellow spring and summer flowers. Also stalks.
Rhus *sumac*. Foliage.
Rose. Many colours, summer flowers.
Rubus *blackberry*. Foliage.
Solidago *golden rod*. Yellow summer flowers.
Sorbus aria *whitebeam*. Foliage.
Trifolium *clover, trefoil*. Pink or white summer flowers. Also foliage and stalks.
Tulipa *tulip*. Many colours, spring flowers.
Vicia *vetch*. Mauve summer flowers.
Viola *violet, pansy, Johnny-jump-up*. Many colours, spring and summer flowers.
Vitis *Virginia creeper*. Foliage.

Ironing

Acer *maple*.
Aesculus *horse chestnut or buckeye*.
Aspidistra lurida *parlour palm*.
Codiaeum *croton*.
Crocosmia crocosmiiflora *montbretia*.
Fagus *beech*.
Gladiolus.
Grasses. All flatter varieties.
Rhus *sumac*.
Quercus *oak*.

Desiccants

Althaea *hollyhock*. Summer.
Anemone. Many colours.
Azalea. Many colours.
Calendula *pot marigold*. Yellow or orange.
Camellia. White, pink or red.
Clematis. Many colours.
Daffodil. Yellow flowers.
Dahlia. Many colours.
Delphinium. Many colours.
Dianthus *carnation, pink*.
Forsythia. Yellow flowers.
Gerbera *Transvaal daisy, Barbarton daisy*.
Yellow, orange or red flowers.
Helleborus *Christmas and Lenten rose*. White,
dark red or green flowers.
Hyacinth. Many colours.
Nymphaea *water lily*. White, yellow or pink.
Orchid. Many colours.
Paeonia *peony*. Yellow, red or white flowers.
Primula *primrose*. Many colours.
Rose. Many colours.
Syringa *lilac*. White or mauve flowers.
Tulipa *tulip*. Many colours.
Viola *violet, pansy*. Many colours.
Zinnia. Many colours.

Glycerine

Acer pseudoplatanus *sycamore*. Foliage and
fruits.
Adiantum *maidenhair fern*. Foliage.
Aspidistra lurida *parlour palm*. Foliage.
Aucuba *spotted laurel*. Foliage.

Bergenia. Foliage.
Buxus *box*. Foliage.
Camellia. Foliage.
Castanea sativa *Spanish chestnut*. Foliage.
Choisya ternata *Mexican orange*. Foliage.
Clematis vitalba *old man's beard*. Seed heads.
Convallaria majalis *lily of the valley*. Foliage.
Cotoneaster. Foliage.
Digitalis *foxglove*. Flowers.
Dipsacus fullonum *teasel*. Seed heads.
Dracaena. Foliage.
Eryngium *sea holly*. Flowers.
Eucalyptus. Foliage.
Fagus *beech*. Foliage.
Fatshedera. Foliage.
Fatsia japonica. Foliage.
Ferns. All varieties. Foliage.
Ficus elastica *rubber plant*. Foliage.
Grevillea robusta *silk oak*. Foliage.
Hedera *ivy*. Foliage.
Helleborus *Christmas or Lenten rose*. Foliage.
Hydrangea. Flowers.
Laurus nobilis *bay*. Foliage.
Magnolia grandiflora *southern magnolia*.
Foliage.
Molucella laevis *bells of Ireland, shell flower*.
Flowers.
Paeonia *peony*. Foliage.
Polygonatum odoratum *Solomon's seal*.
Flowers and foliage.
Quercus *oak*. Foliage.
Rhododendron. Foliage.
Rose. Foliage.
Sorbus aria *whitebeam*. Foliage.
Tilia *linden*. Flowers.

Index

Acknowledgements

Arrangers

Stella Coe: pp. 153, 159, 160, 163–65
Elms Ltd.; 3 Craven Terrace, London W2: p. 127
Sue Frankland: pp. 202–3
Deana at Lennie's, 414 King's Road, London SW10: p. 177
Susan Gaskell: pp. 173, 189
Juliet Glyn Smith: pp. 72, 73 (bottom), 74–77, 83, 85, 87, 88, 90–91, 95, 97, 99, 123
David Hicks: pp. 22–23, 30–31, 59, 63, 67, 71, 73 (top), 78–81, 93, 100, 181, 186, 192–93
Hillier and Hilton Ltd.; 61 Church Road, London SW13: pp. 115, 130–31, 134–39, 141, 143, 174, 179, 199
Frances Kempt: pp. 24, 116–17, 119, 126, 128–29
Hazel Perryman-Bensley: pp. 182–83, 214–15
Daphne Ramsbottom: pp. 25, 27, 52, 103–4, 106, 109–12, 146–49
Kenneth Turner: pp. 120–22, 124, 125, 169, 185, 190, 194–95, 196–97, 200
Pamela Woods: p. 205

Authors

Chapters 1 and 2, Iain Finlayson
Chapters 3 and 8, Anne Johnson
Chapter 4, Charlotte Edwards
Chapter 5, Rosemary Lamont
Chapters 6 and 7, Judy Allen

Locations

pp. 24, 116, 117, 118–19, 126, 128–29 Claridges Hotel, Brook Street, London W1
pp. 25, 106–107, 109, 111, 113 Great Fosters Hote, Egham, Surrey
pp. 34–35 Interior of Hiller and Hilton Ltd., 61 Church Road, London SW13
p. 27 Royal Horticultural Society Gardens, Wisley, Surrey
pp. 167–68 Interior of Kenneth Turner Flowers Ltd., 7 Avery Row, London W1

Illustrators

Yvonne Commander: pp. 206–13
Barbara Firth: pp. 105, 117, 136, 138–43
Vana Haggerty: pp. 26, 36, 40, 158, 161, 162, 164–65, 168, 184, 204
Trevor Lawrence: p. 29
Ken Stott: pp. 33, 41, 44–48, 50–51, 63, 62, 123, 154, 155–56, 176, 191, 201

Flower Paintings

p. 9—a detail from *The Annunciation* by Duccio
p. 10—two details from the *Immaculate Conception* by Crivelli
p. 11—*Paradise Garden* by the Master of the Upper Rhine; the Städel, Frankfurt, Germany
p. 12—by Jean-Baptiste Monnoyer
p.13—by Nicholas Verendael
pp. 15, 16—by Jan van Juysum
p. 17—(top) Jacob Walscappelle (bottom) Rachel Ruysch
p. 18—both pictures by Fantin-Latour
p. 19—Otto Scholderer
p. 60–61—Henri Matisse

Miscellaneous

p. 54—pottery vases from The Craftsmen Potters Association, William Blake House, Marshall Street, London W1
p. 55—glass vases from a selection at David Hicks Ltd., 101 Jermyn Street, London W1
p. 127—china from House of Chinacraft, 198, Regent Street, London W1
p. 138–39—wedding dress and bridesmaid's dress from a selection at Ellis Bridals, Elsley House, 22–30 Great Titchfield Street, London W1